VEGGIE
FROM THE
START

VEGGIE
FROM THE
START

Easy Vegan and Vegetarian Foods
for Babies and Up

RACHEL BOYETT

THE EXPERIMENT
NEW YORK

The Experiment, LLC
220 East 23rd Street, Suite 600
New York, NY 10010-4658
theexperimentpublishing.com

This book contains the opinions and ideas of its author. It is intended to provide helpful and informative material on the subjects addressed in the book. It is sold with the understanding that the author and publisher are not engaged in rendering medical, health, or any other kind of personal professional services in the book. The author and publisher specifically disclaim all responsibility for any liability, loss, or risk—personal or otherwise—that is incurred as a consequence, directly or indirectly, of the use and application of any of the contents of this book.

The Experiment's books are available at special discounts when purchased in bulk for premiums and sales promotions as well as for fund-raising or educational use. For details, contact us at info@theexperimentpublishing.com.

Library of Congress Cataloging-in-Publication Data available upon request

ISBN 978-1-61519-691-3
Ebook ISBN 978-1-61519-692-0

Cover design by Beth Bugler
Text design by Louise Evans

Manufactured in China

First printing October 2020
10 9 8 7 6 5 4 3 2 1

CONTENTS

GETTING STARTED

ABOUT ME

What should be the first foods that you give your children? And is it an extra problem if you are vegetarian or vegan?

In this book, I want to share my experiences of weaning children on vegetarian foods; the recipes are for meals and snacks that I prepared for my two older children. This is the book I wish I'd had by my side at the time, especially when weaning for the first time!

I set up an Instagram account called Little Veggie Eats back in 2015 as a way of documenting my son's weaning journey. I had just emerged from the first 6 months of motherhood, which, like for many, passed in a blur. While I was enjoying being a mother I was finding many aspects of it pretty monotonous—changing, feeding, baby classes, sleeping (a bit!) . . . on repeat. I put off weaning until my son was exactly 6 months old, anticipating disruption to our carefully balanced routine, but also more monotony!

"It turns out I was wrong to dread weaning!"

It ended up being my favorite stage of parenting so far and it inadvertently ended up shaping a career change.

I've always loved food and cooking. Several strong women in my family, my grandmother, sister, and aunt, set me up for a lifetime love of food. Yet during the new-baby haze I'd become disconnected from the enjoyable side of cooking; I had less time to cook, I wasn't experimenting much, and I was "fueling" rather than enjoying food.

I made the decision quite early on that I wasn't going to offer traditional "baby food" to my children. I was interested in offering my son normal food that was suitable for the whole family but at the same time was "baby-friendly." Weaning reconnected me with my enjoyment of cooking and family eating. I had my own human guinea pig to test new creations on and I relished cooking without sugar and salt, and finding ways to create food that was as nutrient-dense as possible.

My husband and I made the decision together to raise our children vegetarian—it was a quick conversation shortly before our first child was born. I've been a vegetarian my whole life and having never cooked meat it wasn't something I was prepared to start doing. I had a very healthy vegetarian childhood so I took it for granted that my son wouldn't need meat to be healthy.

But other people seemed to have a different opinion. I've been told that it wasn't my place to make that decision and my son should decide to be vegetarian when older, if he wanted.

However, we looked at it from the other way around: Why shouldn't we make that decision now, and let him be free to decide otherwise when older? As parents we make hundreds of decisions that shape the way we raise our young children, from what books they read, what TV shows they watch (or if they watch TV at all), what clothes they wear, whether they follow a religion, and if you are meat-eaters, what meat they should eat, and so on.

Being responsible for the health of another (much more vulnerable!) human made me more aware of nutrition in my own diet. I started looking into what nutrients vegetarians need, the different plant-based sources of protein, iron, and calcium, and what foods are nutritionally better than others.

The recipes in this book are intended to be used from the very start of weaning, but with simple adaptations and ingredient tweaks they are for the whole family to enjoy, including older children and adults.

I won't pretend my children haven't gone through fussy phases. They haven't eaten nutritionally dense food for every single meal. But I have always tried to experiment and to introduce them to lots of new flavors and textures. I have never stopped offering them foods even if they might have rejected them, sometimes for months on end.

"I strongly believe that as parents our job is to offer our children a varied diet."

We should do our best to ensure that what they are eating has a good nutritional spread and to be aware of what we are feeding them. And there is no more important time to start this than when your baby first starts eating solids. They might not be eating loads at this stage but they are always learning, always experiencing new things, and in particular, they are entering the world of food.

The recipes are simple, because with the best will in the world, when you have small children life is complicated enough without making cooking challenging, too! These are all recipes my family has enjoyed time and time again. Lots of variety, lots of color, and, above all, an emphasis on putting vegetables at the heart of the family table.

VEGETARIAN & PLANT-BASED DIETS

"As someone who has been a vegetarian my whole life, I have seen attitudes and awareness change dramatically over the years."

When I was a child, being a vegetarian was something of an oddity. Not any more! I am overjoyed that a collective awakening seems to be happening. It makes eating out, shopping, and cooking much easier; there are more recipes, more ingredients, and more options than ever before!

Traditionally, someone who follows a vegetarian diet does not eat meat, fish, or chicken. If you are following a vegan or a plant-based diet, you also don't eat any animal products including milk, cheese, eggs, and honey. Although I'm not vegan myself, lots of the recipes in this book are either vegan or easily adapted to be vegan. This is to do with a general shift in my household toward reducing animal products where possible, but also because while I've been running Little Veggie Eats on Instagram I would often be asked to suggest alternatives for people whose babies had allergies to dairy or egg.

There seems to be a more fluid approach to labels based on what we eat now, and this is no bad thing. It is perfectly acceptable to eat a vegan diet Monday to Friday, or to be vegetarian at home but not when eating out, or just to be trying to eat less meat and dairy whenever you can. Some people think that the so-called "flexitarian" diet is very much the diet of the future. If it encourages people to reduce the animal products they eat, then it is a positive step.

You might be reading this book because you are new to vegetarianism or veganism and want to know how you can bring your child up with the same diet. Or you might just be committed to eating a little less meat and animal products and want your child to do the same. Whatever you do, and however you've labeled yourself, ultimately we all just want the best for our children and for them to grow up enjoying a healthy relationship with food.

CLIMATE CHANGE & THE FUTURE OF FOOD

Each generation is different from the previous one. Whatever our own food preferences and eating history, it seems a safe bet that our children will not be eating in the same way as we did as kids.

We are headed toward a climate disaster and scientists keep saying that dramatic changes to our global diet are needed. The key point is that we need to eat fewer animal products due to the environmental impact of intensive animal farming. That will mean increasing the amount of plant-based foods we eat. By starting your baby on a meat-reduced or meat-free diet, you are equipping them for the world in which they will have to live.

NUTRITION

You will find information in this book on what your baby needs nutritionally as they start eating solid food, a rough timeline on how weaning might look for your baby, and tips and tricks for calm and relaxed weaning. I worked closely with the book's consultant nutritionist, Jodie Abrahams, to understand a baby's nutritional needs and how these can be met with a vegetarian or plant-based diet. The nutritional information given throughout the book should give you confidence that the food you are making is meeting your baby's needs.

You might be concerned about your baby getting the nutrients they need from their vegetarian diet. A common concern is that they might not get enough variety, iron, or protein.

I think that our children have eaten a much larger variety of foods because we are vegetarian; I am way more conscious of offering them as many different legumes, seeds, and vegetables as possible as I know that they need to eat a variety of foods to ensure they are getting all their essential nutrients.

It is very easy to ensure your child gets all the protein and iron that they need on a vegetarian diet. Legumes, nuts, seeds, dairy, and eggs all provide protein and iron, and by combining these with lots of veggies you can help your baby's body get the most out of the nutrients. If you want to bring your child up vegan, or your child has dairy or egg allergies, then you will need a bit more planning and consideration to ensure all your child's nutritional needs are met, maybe even considering some supplements. There is more detailed information on nutrition on pages 32–35.

IS A PLANT-BASED DIET HARD WORK?

There is always so much to do with young children. If you are new to a vegetarian or vegan diet, the thought of adding to your pressures will be worrying, especially as weaning your baby can be daunting enough. It will be easy to say: "I'll wait until my child is used to eating solid foods before introducing them to a special diet." But will vegetarian weaning add to your workload? The short answer (and the long answer. . .) is no! All of my recipes are quick and easy to prepare. I'm a busy parent myself and as much as I would love to have lots of time for cooking, I do not. It can also be quicker than cooking meat!

You will see my recipes generally include short cuts, for instance, using canned cooked legumes. If you have time to soak and cook dried legumes, or are used to doing that already, then that's great, but it's not necessary for these recipes.

IS A VEGETARIAN OR PLANT-BASED DIET MORE EXPENSIVE?

Definitely not! Nuts and seeds can be quite expensive, as can good organic tofu as well as some of the speciality grains, but they are still cheaper than ethically bred meat.

There are also ways to keep costs down, and here are a few tips:

Buy in bulk
If you can, buying larger packages can save costs on foods with a fairly long shelf life, for example nuts, seeds, grains, and shelf-stable foods like quinoa.

Buy in season
I try to buy organic food where I can but this tends to be more expensive than nonorganic produce. This is because fewer pesticides and fertilizers are used in the growing process. Buying vegetables that are in season is a great way

to reduce costs (and is also better for the environment as your food comes with a lower carbon footprint). I am a member of a local vegetable program where I collect seasonal organic vegetables each week. This is a cost-effective way of buying locally grown organic vegetables.

Buy frozen fruit and veggies

I also frequently buy frozen fruit and vegetables such as raspberries, peas, corn, edamame beans, and many more; they are generally frozen very soon after they are picked as this helps to lock in valuable nutrients. The shopping list on page 17 lists the frozen produce I often buy.

COOKING GUIDANCE

USING THIS BOOK

I have written the recipes as I've cooked them for my family, often with kids underfoot! All the recipes are straightforward and don't need too much advance planning; when one does I've tried to make that very clear (I've been caught off guard by the buried "now leave for two hours" instruction in a recipe far too many times).

Most of the recipes can be easily adapted to what you have in stock and what's readily available at the grocery store. As I try to eat seasonally I find the vegetables in my recipes change throughout the year, so I've included some variation tips when there is space.

You'll find that recipes are marked with the following symbols to let you see at a glance if they:

 involve no cooking   freeze well

 are ideal first foods   are best for 8 months plus

MEASUREMENTS

Quite often a recipe will mention a "handful" of something. Don't worry about getting this wrong—I've used this measurement when you don't need to be exact. The same applies when I've said you need to add a vegetable but there's no size—if I've not specified then assume it's a regular-sized vegetable of its kind. If it needs to be precise I'll say.

My recipes use cups as well as metric measurements. Cups are ideal for cooking on limited time as you don't need to worry about getting out a scale (and there's less to wash!).

KITCHEN EQUIPMENT

I've tried not to use too much complicated and expensive equipment, but the following are pretty essential:

- **Food processor or blender**. You can buy small, basic models that do the job; I use a Nutribullet, which is very straightforward, powerful, and quick to wash afterward.

- **Muffin baking pan** for the muffins and individual bars. I use a 12-cup muffin pan for all my recipes, although you don't always need to use all the cups!
- **Ice cube tray** for freezing individual portions of sauce
- **Steamer**. You can get a basic steamer to use on the stove over a pan, a standalone, or a microwave version. They are great for cooking vegetables quickly so they don't lose their nutrients

KEY INGREDIENTS

I've found the key to quick, nutritious vegetarian and vegan cooking is getting your kitchen cupboards stocked with some key ingredients. Here are some of my favorites that I suggest you stock up on:

Oats
Oats are a great slow-release carbohydrate so they will keep your baby fuller for longer. They are also high in fiber and soothing on digestion (especially important as you might find your baby gets constipated as their stomach adapts to solid food).

Spinach / leafy greens
High in vitamins and minerals including iron, vitamins C and K, and folate, spinach and dark leafy greens provide a number of important nutrients. The texture of leafy greens can be a bit challenging for babies when they start weaning so I'm a big fan of blending and finely chopping green vegetables to make it easier for babies to get a taste for them (and to get used to the color).

Eggs
The humble egg packs in a lot of nutritional qualities and is a great source of protein. Scrambled egg, omelette, hard-boiled eggs . . . all can be ready in minutes and are wonderfully nutritious for your baby. I always try to buy organic, free-range eggs and although more expensive, they are still much cheaper than meat.

There are some great alternatives to egg if your baby can't eat them or you are following a vegan diet (see page 182 for alternatives).

Lentils and chickpeas

This wouldn't be a vegetarian recipe book without an abundance of legumes. Lentils and chickpeas will always be my favorites as they are so versatile. They are a brilliant source of protein and iron. Dried and cooked are both great options; I use canned varieties a lot for speed.

Pumpkin and squash

Pumpkin and squash are perfect first-food vegetables. They go soft when cooked so are very easy to mash for spoon-feeding and to offer in finger food batons for baby-led weaning.

Milk and yogurt

My children do not follow a dairy-free diet and they eat a lot of natural yogurt. I use yogurt a lot to serve alongside fruit and savory dishes. It's packed with useful fats, essential for your baby's brain development and to help with vitamin absorption. It also contains calcium, which is essential for healthy bones, and vitamin B12 for good nerve health. I always buy full-fat natural yogurt with no added sugar, and organic if possible.

There are lots of dairy-free yogurts on the market if your baby has a dairy allergy or you are following a vegan diet. See pages 180–181 for more information on dairy-free alternatives.

All references to "milk" and "yogurt" in the recipes can be any milk or yogurt of your choice. I really like oat milk (choose one with a fat content equivalent to full-fat cow's milk) and coconut yogurt.

Nuts and seeds

Rich in protein and essential fats, nuts and seeds are an amazing way to add taste and nutrition to vegetarian and vegan diets. Before offering nuts and seeds to your baby, read the allergy advice on page 29. If your baby has a peanut, tree nut, or seed allergy refer to page 183 for alternatives.

As nuts and seeds have different nutritional benefits it's good to buy a wide variety. For example, walnuts are a good source of vitamin E and omega-3 fats, and almonds and sesame seeds are high in calcium.

SHOPPING LIST

These are the foods I generally have in my cupboards at home:

Staples
- Whole wheat flour
- Chickpea flour
- Quinoa
- Pasta
- Brown rice
- Noodles
- Ground almonds
- Whole nuts such as cashews, walnuts, and hazelnuts
- Seeds such as sunflower, pumpkin, chia, hulled hemp, poppy, sesame, and flax
- Dessicated coconut
- Oats
- Baking powder
- Nutritional yeast
- Olive oil
- Coconut oil
- Toasted sesame oil
- Balsamic vinegar

Cans
- Coconut milk
- Chopped tomatoes
- Brown lentils
- Chickpeas
- Black beans

Seasonings
- Cinnamon
- Ground coriander
- Ground cumin
- Sweet paprika
- Pumpkin pie spice
- Garlic granules or powder

Fridge
- Milk (full-fat dairy and oat milk)
- Plain full-fat natural yogurt (dairy and coconut)
- Nut butters such as peanut, cashew, and almond
- Tahini
- Lemon
- Garlic
- Ginger

Freezer
- Spinach
- Peas
- Edamame beans
- Corn
- Raspberries
- Blueberries
- Cherries

BASIC PANTRY RECIPES

The following are some simple methods that I use throughout the book.

Milling nuts and seeds

Little seeds such as sesame, chia, hulled hemp, and poppy can be left whole in recipes, but larger nuts and seeds should be milled or crushed before use as they can be a choking hazard.

It's very easy to mill nuts and seeds at home if you have a blender, just pulse them until they are a crumble or powder. As your baby gets older you can gradually leave the seeds and nuts a little chunkier. If you don't have a blender you can use a pestle and mortar to grind them, or place the seeds or nuts in a freezer bag and bash with a rolling pin until they are crushed.

Oat flour

Making your own oat flour couldn't be easier! Just put a couple of cups of oats in the blender and pulse until they are a powder. Store in an airtight jar.

Salt-free stock

If you want completely salt-free veggie stock, then try making your own! It's also an amazing way of using veggie scraps and peelings. Use a container in the freezer to collect scraps and peelings of veggies as you use them. The best bits to save are: onions, celery, carrots, and mushroom stems. When the container is full, toss the scraps in a saucepan and cover with water. Add some sprigs of herbs if you have them: thyme, rosemary, and bay leaves are good. Bring the water to a boil and then simmer for 1–2 hours until the water looks like stock or broth. Using a sieve to catch the scraps, pour the stock into a mixing bowl. Then either freeze this or continue to cook it down until it is very thick. You can then freeze the stock in an ice cube tray and use when you need it.

TIME-SAVING TIPS & TRICKS

When you have a baby you quickly lose control of a lot of your time. Most of my recipes are quick to do or once you have done the prep, you can leave it to cook. However, I know all too well that some days even finding 20 minutes to prepare some food can be a struggle. This is why it can be very helpful to get into the habit of batch-cooking, making a freezer stash, and freezing leftovers when you do have some spare time. Here are some prep suggestions that you can do when you have a spare half an hour or less:

- Make a batch of muffins (see page 80) or crackers (see page 91)
- Throw together a dip for use during the week (see pages 96–103)
- Make some veggie-loaded tomato sauce to freeze into portions for extra quick meals (see page 105)
- Chop and roast some veggies
- Cook some grains such as quinoa, rice, or bulgur wheat, which you can keep in the fridge and use for Buddha bowls (see pages 109–119)
- Prepare a breakfast that can be made ahead of time such as overnight oats (see page 40), or a pancake mix (see page 43)

YOUR FREEZER STASH

You'll find me talking a lot about a "freezer stash" in the book. Building up a freezer stash is the best way to ensure you have quick access to lots of nutritious foods on those days when you don't feel like cooking or when you just haven't got time. It's also great to load your freezer with food and snacks for lunch on the go—grab some in the morning if you are going out for the day.

- Use ice cube trays to freeze individual portions of sauces. Once they are frozen, you can pop them out and put them in a larger freezer container or bag ready to use. I always have some pesto (see page 94) or veggie-loaded tomato sauce (see page 105) in the freezer for quick meals; they are perfect stirred into pasta or with any of the quick meal hacks on pages 136–137 and 148–149.
- Freeze any leftover pancakes and muffins. Take them out of the freezer in the evening and they'll be defrosted by breakfast (or take out in the morning and they'll be defrosted by lunch).
- Some of the main meals are deliberately over-generous for the average-sized family. This is so leftovers can be frozen! Portion them out into small baby-size portions and you'll have instant freezer meals.

COOKING VEGGIES

Low-temperature roasting or steaming can help to retain the maximum nutrients from vegetables. For example, vitamin C is lost through cooking, so lightly steaming vitamin C–rich veggies like leafy greens, broccoli, peas, peppers, sweet potato, and carrots is a good way of minimizing how much is lost.

To roast veggies, cut them into batons, drizzle with oil (I tend to use olive oil), and roast at 350°F (180°C) for around 30 minutes. Potatoes and root veggies might need a little longer—you can use a fork to check if they are soft enough.

How long veggies take to steam depends on which type of steamer you use and the nature of the veggies. There are stove-top ones (which fit in a regular pan), standalone ones, and microwave ones. A microwave steamer will generally be the quickest at cooking veggies.

STORE-BOUGHT BABY FOOD

Yes, my children have store-bought food from time to time. Baby food pouches can be a lifesaver when you are caught short out and about, traveling, or sick. I used pouches for pasta sauces when I was in the depths of morning sickness with my second and my freezer stash had run out.

When you do use store-bought baby food it's a good idea to check the labels. I choose jars that don't use fruit fillers (i.e. high levels of fruit to sweeten savory food) and have short ingredient lists (or at least lists where I recognize all the ingredients).

Remember that designated "baby snacks" like rice cakes are not very nutritionally dense. If you do use them, adding something like nut butter, hummus, or cream cheese will help increase the nutrition.

I have never used baby oatmeal or baby rice; I just used normal rice and oatmeal. If I felt my children needed them smoother, then I milled the oats first, or blended the finished rice dish. It is much cheaper, not to mention more convenient, to have your baby eating what you eat.

INTRODUCING YOUR BABY TO SOLID FOOD

"It's normal to have mixed emotions about weaning."

Introducing your baby to solid food is one of those big first steps where you start preparing them for their life beyond being a baby. You might be excited or you might be worried about it.

It's normal to have mixed emotions about weaning. You might be worried it is going to disrupt your routine. Yes, it is a big change, it is messy, and at first it can feel challenging to fit food into your day. But it is also amazing seeing your baby discover new tastes and textures (and forming their own preferences!).

WHEN TO START WEANING & SIGNS OF READINESS

Current American Academy of Pediatrics advice is to start weaning when your baby is around 6 months old. Before 6 months your baby is able to get all their nutrients from breast milk or formula milk. Waiting until 6 months means that your baby's digestive system will be better able to deal with food, they will be able to feed themselves, and be better able to chew and move food around their mouths. In practical terms, this means that you will find your baby can quickly progress to eating food suitable for the whole family (which is a big time saver).

There are three signs that your baby is ready to start weaning:

1. They are able to sit up and hold their heads steady.
2. They can coordinate their eyes, hands, and mouth so they can look at their food, pick it up, and put it in their mouth.
3. They are able to swallow food (rather than spit it back out).

Although I refer to "weaning" throughout this book to refer to introducing your baby to solid foods, I actually prefer the term "complementary feeding" when talking about introducing babies to food between 6 and 12 months. This is because during this time breast milk or formula still provides the vast majority of the nutrients that your baby needs. This is especially helpful to remember if your baby doesn't take as quickly to food.

WHAT TO AVOID WHEN WEANING

Salt

Babies only need a very small amount of salt in their diet a day (less than 1 g of salt/less than 0.4 g sodium). As salt occurs in many products you offer to your baby already, such as bread and cheese, there is no need to add any further salt in their diet (this includes adding salt to cooking water). Be sure to buy cans of beans and legumes in unsalted water.

When cooking for young children, always use very low-salt bouillon cubes in cooking, or homemade vegetable stock (see page 18).

Honey

Honey is not suitable for babies under 12 months as honey can contain bacteria that can lead to infant botulism.

Sugar

Your baby doesn't need processed sugar and it is not good for their teeth (which might be just coming through!). Processed or added sugar tends to be empty calories and does not have much nutritional benefit.

As well as standard sugar I also avoid sugar replacement syrups like maple syrup and date syrup for babies under 12 months. Throughout this book I use naturally sweet veggies and fruit (which contain naturally occurring sugars) to provide sweetness in dishes.

Over-processed packaged food

Packaged food generally contains high levels of salt and sugar, so rather than continually checking labels for salt and sugar levels it's much easier to avoid them. This is especially true for lots of meat-substitute products, where the salt levels are really high.

Rather than looking to meat substitutes, instead think about offering your baby lots of legumes, eggs, and tofu. Tofu can be tricky for young children to digest, so offer in moderation as part of a varied diet, and I suggest organic, high-quality tofu.

DRINKS

Your baby's main drink will still be breast milk or formula. Offer your baby water along with their meal in a suitable cup.

Although you can use cow's milk or dairy-free milk in cooking you should not offer them as a drink until your baby is over 12 months.

SPOON-FED & BABY-LED WEANING

The two main types of weaning that people discuss are spoon-fed weaning and baby-led weaning.

Spoon-fed weaning
This is probably how you were weaned! The idea is that babies are fed smooth, puréed food by spoon, with lumps and more texture gradually added over time.

Baby-led weaning
Baby-led weaning is when babies feed themselves. You offer finger food for them to pick up and put in their mouth. Babies are capable of gumming lots of different foods before they get teeth so they are able to suck and explore food for themselves.

The main rationale behind baby-led weaning is giving the baby freedom to choose what and how much they eat.

My approach is somewhere in the middle of spoon-fed and baby-led. I'm a big fan of following your child's lead and tuning in to what works for them.

Recent research suggests that the way you wean your baby does not have any measurable impact on fussiness later down the line. So watch your baby, see what they are enjoying, what's working for them and let them teach you how they want to be weaned.

ACTUAL FOOD NOT BABY FOOD

Family mealtimes are really important to me. Growing up we always sat around the dinner table to eat as a family. I was never excited about feeding my children "baby food," but I was excited about sharing mealtimes with them.

My approach to weaning has always been to offer regular food made suitable for a baby. We eat plenty of food ourselves (like dips!) that are blended and smooth so to me this seemed perfect for a baby. Lots of the food that I've marked as ideal first foods in the recipes fall into this category.

All of the recipes in the book are ones that I hope you can all enjoy as a family. If your baby sees you eating something, they are more likely to eat it themselves. Rather than cooking them something separate, make everyone the same food, and then make adaptations on how you serve it (or what you add at the end).

NUTRITIONALLY DENSE

Babies have very small stomachs so they don't need to eat much before they become full. Because of this it's important to try to ensure that what they are eating is rich in the nutrients that meet their needs.

Wherever possible I think about what swaps can be made to traditional food to give it a better nutritional profile. This not only benefits your baby, but the whole family, too.

VEGGIE-LOADED NOT HIDDEN

I'm a big believer in getting babies to love veggies for what they are. This means offering them lots of batons of veggies alongside the puréed or mashed version.

I do appreciate that some of the recipes in this book look as though I am trying to hide veggies (like Rainbow Pancakes, Green Eggs, veggies in Ice Pops, etc.). In my opinion there is a huge distinction between blending in the veggies to "hide" them and blending them in to enhance the color and flavor of your food.

I use squash, sweet potato, and carrot a lot in dishes to add natural sweetness, flavor, and nutrients. A traditional tomato sauce generally contains sugar to counteract the acidity of the tomato, and instead I use carrots or sweet potato.

Spinach and beets are my color enhancers of choice. The pink you get in smoothies or ice pops by adding beets is amazing. The same goes for spinach in smoothies or in eggs. And, of course, the nutritional benefits of adding veggies really makes it a no-brainer.

TIPS FOR RELAXED & SUCCESSFUL WEANING

"The success
of a mealtime
is not just
measured
by what gets
eaten."

The most important thing you should aim to do during weaning is to help your baby build a good relationship with nutritious food.

Food prep

Expose your baby to prepping and making food right from the start! Sitting your baby in the kitchen watching you cook is all valuable food exposure. And it won't be long before they are ready to help (a toddler in the kitchen is messy but fun!).

Variety

Eating a varied diet is the best way to ensure we get all the nutrients our body needs. This is especially true when you have a vegetarian or plant-based diet. Different vegetables, nuts, seeds, and legumes all have different nutritional profiles and by eating a wide selection your baby has a better chance of meeting their nutritional requirements.

Babies' preferences are often based on what they know best. So the more food they see, the more likely they will end up enjoying it. It can take a baby over 10 times of trying something to decide if they actually like or dislike it, so don't give up even if they don't seem receptive to a new flavor!

No distractions

Sitting around a dinner table with the family eating, with no distractions (e.g., no screens!) shows your baby that mealtimes are relaxing and enjoyable.

All eating the same

Babies copy and mimic us. It's not just time-saving to all eat the same food but it also signals to your baby that this is the food to eat, and you enjoy it, too.

Positive language

Although your baby is still small try to use positive language around food—this will get you into a good habit for when they are older.

A good friend of mine told me she never spoke with her children about "not liking" something, but instead would say: "Oh you don't feel like it today." This is something I copied and found really helpful. Babies and young children can be quite fickle in their tastes, so it's best never to cement anything with words.

The sensory experience

Touching and playing with food is all part of the weaning process. Even if nothing is going in their mouth, your baby is learning new motor skills and becoming aware of different textures and sensations.

I've tried to incorporate lots of different colors into the food in this book. Bright colors encourage your baby to engage, touch, and taste their food.

Follow your baby's cues

If your baby is turning their head away from a spoon, pushing it away, or clamping their mouth closed they don't want any more. Don't force them to eat (even if they haven't eaten anything). Likewise with finger food, if they lose interest move on from the mealtime. If they are still happy playing with food, even if they aren't eating, let them continue to explore until they are bored.

You don't want food to become a battleground or mealtimes to become a negative experience for your baby.

Portion size

It's impossible to set a portion size amount for a baby as their appetites can change so much from day to day. You might also find that the majority of finger food ends up on the floor so in reality you are offering them far more food than they will ever eat.

Don't get hung up on how much your baby is eating. Some days they might have a few teaspoons of something, other days they might not try anything.

Embrace the mess

Yes, weaning is messy, especially if you opt for baby-led weaning, but that's not a bad thing! Invest in a good dustpan and brush, some rags, and maybe an overall-style bib and go with it.

Teething can upset everything

Teething can be really tough for babies and can dramatically impact their appetite, mood, and sleep (yours and theirs). Offer them food but never force it. Things like ice pops and nice cream (see pages 161 and 169) and yogurt might be soothing for their sore mouth. Or they might prefer cold batons of veggies (cucumber is great) or a hard cracker (like Chickpea Crackers on page 91) to gnaw on. Experiment, but don't be disheartened if they only want milk—it's totally normal.

KNOW THE DIFFERENCE BETWEEN GAGGING & CHOKING

A common concern I hear is that people think their baby is choking on finger food or lumpy food. It is likely they are just gagging. Familiarize yourself with the differences:

Gagging is a natural part of weaning as your baby learns to eat and move solids around their mouth. It's all part of the learning process. However, if your baby gets very upset by gagging you might want to try offering less lumpy food.

Signs of gagging include:

- Coughing or retching
- Eyes watering
- Bringing food back up

Choking is more serious and is a sign that something is lodged in your baby's airway. If your baby is choking they will be silent as they struggle to breathe.

To reduce the risk of choking:

- Avoid those foods that can block airways, such as chunks of food that could be swallowed whole, for example, chunks of cheese, apple, or raw carrot
- Always cut grapes in half lengthwise

- Chop cherry tomatoes in half
- Squish large blueberries and beans before offering them
- Don't offer whole nuts—crush them first (see page 18)

Always supervise your baby when they are eating.

WEANING EQUIPMENT

Contrary to what the stores would have you believe, you don't need much equipment to get you started. When your baby first starts weaning you will either be feeding them with a spoon or offering them finger food.

- A couple of small baby spoons
- A couple of small bowls. You can use bowls you already have as long as they can withstand a lot of throwing on the floor!
- High chair. You want your baby to be supported and safe while they are eating. Making sure they are sitting upright helps to avoid choking. There are many high chairs on the market and you don't need to spend a fortune. My own high chair wish list had two requirements: Is it easy to clean? Can I sit the baby at the table with it?
- Cup or sippy cup to offer water in

The following are all things I have found helpful throughout weaning, but they are by no means essential:

- Small portable rubber feeding mat, which I would put finger food on (we also used it when going out)
- Reusable pouches. I found these really great for yogurt, dips, and smoothies on the go.
- Bento box with a good seal. A decent bento box meant I could take a selection of different foods out. If you get a good one this will hopefully last your baby for a long time.

ALLERGY ADVICE

"It's very normal to be worried about allergies when you start weaning."

Allergies are pretty common in children and many have more than one. Generally, as children's immune systems develop, they outgrow allergies (although allergies to foods that cause severe reactions are more likely to last). A true food allergy is when the body's immune system mounts a response to a particular food. Food sensitivities or intolerances are not allergies as such, but can cause symptoms affecting digestion, skin, and behavior, etc.

Most of the time allergic reactions are mild and may include:

- an itchy, red rash, or eczema
- a running nose
- sneezing or itchy
- watering eyes

A more severe (but rarer) reaction is anaphylaxis, which is a medical emergency. Symptoms can include breathing difficulties, flushed or clammy skin, a fast heartbeat, or swelling around the face and throat. Your baby may be at higher risk of food allergies if there is a family history or if they already suffer from conditions such as asthma or eczema. If this is the case, you may want to seek medical advice before introducing allergenic foods.

Don't be put off introducing your baby to potential allergenic foods if you don't have a family history. Instead, offer small amounts of foods one by one and monitor your baby's reaction.

The most common allergens are:

- cow's milk
- eggs
- foods that contain gluten, including wheat, barley, and rye
- tree nuts, peanuts, and seeds
- soy
- shellfish/fish

When you introduce known allergens keep a food journal and note down any reactions. If your baby has any reactions see your pediatrician as soon as possible.

WEANING TIMELINE

Some babies will take to food very quickly and you might find they progress to eating family food after just a few weeks of weaning. Others take a little more time and you might find they are eating softer food with less texture for longer. Try to follow your baby's lead and you'll both find the experience more enjoyable and less stressful.

FIRST TASTES: AROUND 6 MONTHS

Week 1

Start with one meal a day, at a time when your baby is most relaxed and not too tired. Offering about 1 hour before or after a milk feed is usually a good time to start.

Start with simple, less sweet vegetables such as broccoli, zucchini, and cauliflower as research suggests starting with vegetables might mean your baby is more accepting of vegetables in meals later on.

For spoon-feeding: Steam the veggie, add a little water or breast milk/formula and then purée.

For baby-led weaning and mixed weaning: Offer some steamed or roasted veggie batons as finger foods to your baby. If you are baby-led weaning, offer the baton only. Cucumber and avocado can be offered raw.

Week 2

If your baby is over 6 months, start offering starchy foods like rice, oats, and grains, along with sweeter veggies like carrots and squash and legumes such as lentils. Beans and other legumes should be gently mashed or puréed.

If you like you can introduce known allergens such as dairy, eggs, wheat, nuts, and seeds. Offer one new food every 3–4 days so you can see if your baby is OK with them. I'd start with dairy such as yogurt, then eggs (offer yolk and white separately), then wheat (such as pasta or toasted bread), and then nuts and seeds. Offer the new foods in the day so if they react you are not in bed. If your baby doesn't react then incorporate it into your baby's diet. New

research shows that leaving the introduction of allergenic foods—specifically peanuts and hen's eggs—beyond the first 6–12 months of life might actually increase the risk of allergies to those foods.

Weeks 3–4

Start offering fruits. Orange (leave the peel on for easy gripping), melon, mango, banana, and strawberries are good as finger foods. Lightly steam harder fruits like apple and pear.

Consider adding a second meal if your baby is enjoying it, again about an hour before or after a milk feed.

During the first month your baby is unlikely to drop any milk feeds. Keep offering them their usual milk feeds and don't worry if your baby isn't eating much yet.

7–9 MONTHS

Most of the recipes in this book are suitable at this age, although you might want to gently mash or purée the food depending on what texture your baby prefers.

Offer finger foods with every meal (this can be any of the snacks on pages 69–91 or veggie batons).

If you are spoon-feeding start introducing some more texture to the purée.

Offer a variety of food.

Add a third meal to the day when you think your baby is ready so that they are eating breakfast, lunch, and dinner (the time of day that they eat these will vary depending on what works for them and you as a family).

Your baby is still probably having around four milk feeds a day (or more if they feed on demand) but you might start to notice them taking less. All babies are different and some take a bit longer to get used to eating.

10–12 MONTHS

Everything in this book is suitable. You will probably want to stop mashing or puréeing around this point.

Your baby should be on three meals a day. They might also start wanting snacks in between meals (mid-morning and mid-afternoon).

Your baby will be developing their pincer grasp and so will enjoy chasing smaller foods around a plate (e.g., beans, peas, etc. can be left whole for them to pick up).

Start introducing a spoon for them to feed themselves (if you haven't already).

Your baby might have dropped a milk feed and be on three milk feeds a day—or more or less. There are no hard and fast rules!

YOUR BABY'S NUTRITIONAL NEEDS

The biggest question you might have about raising your child with a vegetarian or meat-reduced diet is whether they are missing out on any key nutrients. I consulted with nutritionist Jodie Abrahams to get a run-down on the key nutritional considerations of a vegetarian or plant-based diet.

The foods on your baby's plate will be made up of carbohydrate, fat, and protein, which are known as the "macro-nutrients" (or the building blocks of nutrition). Vitamins and minerals (or "micro-nutrients") contained within these foods are needed in smaller amounts.

VARIETY IS KEY

Don't stress too much about each individual nutrient. As I have said before, the most important thing you can do is offer your child a varied diet and encourage them to continue eating a variety of food as they grow. If you have any particular concerns or want to read more about what your baby needs nutritionally see the resources at the end of this book.

IRON

When your baby hits 6 months old, their iron stores start to diminish. The iron in breast milk is no longer sufficient to meet your baby's needs so it is important to ensure your baby eats iron-rich foods.

Iron is needed for red blood cells to transport oxygen throughout the body and is essential for growth, development, and mental function.

The best-known source of iron is red meat and meat-eaters often question whether a vegetarian diet can give young children enough iron. However, there are lots of good vegetarian sources of iron:

- **Dark green leafy vegetables** like spinach, kale, chard, broccoli, and cabbage
- **Legumes:** lentils, split peas, chickpeas, peas
- **Whole grains:** oats, whole wheat bread, and pasta
- **Nuts:** cashews, almonds, hazelnuts
- **Seeds:** sesame, pumpkin, hemp, quinoa
- **Eggs**
- **Dried fruit:** apricots, raisins, figs

Vitamin C supports iron absorption, so to help your baby get the most iron out of their diet try to include a vitamin-C rich food alongside an iron-rich food. For example, hummus (see page 96) served with a squeeze of lemon and batons of red pepper. Green leafy vegetables are ideal as they combine both!

PROTEIN

You'll often hear people worrying whether you are getting enough protein when you are eating a vegetarian or plant-based diet. All tissues in our bodies—from cells to muscles and organs to bones—need protein in order to be produced, to grow, and to repair.

You might hear people refer to proteins as "complete" proteins; this means they have all the nine amino acids our bodies need to build proteins. The following are good vegetarian and plant-based complete proteins:

- Dairy
- Eggs
- Tofu
- Quinoa
- Buckwheat

The following are good sources of plant-based protein. Although they are not complete proteins, with a varied diet you can combine them to form complete proteins:

- **Legumes:** lentils, chickpeas, split peas, peas, black beans
- **Nuts:** walnuts, cashews, peanuts, almonds
- **Seeds:** sesame, flax, pumpkin, sunflower
- **Whole grains:** brown rice, whole wheat bread

FAT & OMEGAS

Fat is essential for your baby's growth. Fats are needed for neurological development and brain function as well as to absorb vitamins and to produce and regulate hormones. Good sources of vegetarian fats are:

- Avocado and avocado oil
- Coconut oil
- Olive oil
- Full-fat dairy such as cow's milk and yogurt
- Plant-based milks and yogurt (choose milks with a similar high-fat content to cow's milk such as hemp, soy, and oat)
- Nuts
- Seeds

Omega-3 and -6 fatty acids are key for brain and eye health. A varied diet generally provides enough omega-6 fats: they're plentiful in nuts, seeds, whole grains, eggs, and vegetable oils like olive and sunflower.

Omega-3 is slightly trickier as the most readily available form is found in oily fish. Lower quantities of omega-3 are found in walnuts, chia seeds, hemp seeds, and flaxseeds. You can also buy eggs enriched with omega-3. Include these foods in your baby's diet and you may also want to consider a good quality children's omega-3 supplement made from algae oil.

CALCIUM

Calcium is needed to support healthy bones and teeth. If your baby has a dairy allergy your first thought might be—but what about calcium? Don't worry; while dairy is rich in calcium, there are other plant-based sources too, such as:

- Sesame seeds
- Almonds
- Broccoli, cabbage, spinach, and kale
- Egg yolk
- Tofu
- Fortified products like plant-based milks and yogurts (see "Adapting Recipes," page 179)

VITAMIN B12

B12 is needed for healthy cell formation and nerve health. B12 is found naturally in animal products so if you have a fully plant-based diet, try to choose foods that are fortified with B12. You might also want to discuss whether a supplement is needed with your GP or a dietitian. Vegetarian sources of B12 include:

- Dairy
- Eggs
- Fortified grains
- Fortified plant milks
- Nutritional yeast, fortified with B12

ZINC

Zinc plays a key role in boosting immune systems and helping the body fight infections. It's also critical for physical growth and mental development. Good vegetarian sources of zinc are:

- Egg yolks
- Sunflower and pumpkin seeds
- Whole grains: whole wheat flour, brown rice, oats
- Legumes: lentils, chickpeas, beans

IODINE

Iodine helps make thyroid hormones, which are needed to keep cells and metabolic rate healthy. Dairy products are the primary vegetarian source of iodine so if your baby is dairy-free choose iodine-fortified plant-based milk and yogurt. Also speak to your GP or a dietitian about whether supplementation is necessary.

CARBOHYDRATES

Carbohydrates are our primary source of energy. Complex carbohydrates will provide a more steady release of energy and also include fiber. Oats, pasta, bread, rice, buckwheat, quinoa, legumes, and fruit and vegetables (especially starchy ones like sweet and white potatoes, squash, and pumpkin) are all good sources of complex carbohydrates.

VITAMIN C

As well as supporting iron absorption, vitamin C also supports blood cell formation, is critical for immune system function, supports connective tissues, and plays a key role in energy production. Loads of fruit and veggies are rich in vitamin C, but particularly good sources are:

- Dark green leafy veggies (e.g., broccoli, spinach, cabbage, and Brussels sprouts)
- Berries (e.g., raspberries, blueberries, and strawberries)
- Citrus fruits (e.g., oranges, lemons, and limes)
- Papaya
- Peppers
- Pineapples
- Sweet potatoes
- Tomatoes

VITAMIN D

Vitamin D—aka the "sunshine" vitamin— regulates calcium absorption, meaning it's needed for strong bones and teeth as well as heart and muscle function. It's also important for a healthy immune system. The best source of vitamin D is sunlight (or a supplement) but it's also available in small amounts in:

- Butter
- Egg yolks
- Some processed grains and bread, which are fortified with vitamin D

FOLATE

Folate is more commonly known as folic acid or vitamin B9. Folate plays a number of important roles in the body, including growing tissues, helping cells to function, and maturing blood cells.

The best sources are:

- Green leafy vegetables like spinach and broccoli
- Lentils, chickpeas, and black beans

FIBER

Fiber keeps your baby's digestive system healthy and stops them from getting constipated. You should be cautious of giving your baby exclusively whole grains (such as whole grain bread, whole wheat pasta, and brown rice) which are high in fiber; they can fill them up making them too full for other food. As long as you offer a variety of carbohydrates, and don't only offer whole grains, then this is unlikely to happen to your baby.

BREAKFAST & BRUNCH

Breakfast has always been my favorite meal of the day and it was my favorite weaning meal, too. Generally your baby is probably in their best mood in the morning (in contrast to late afternoon when they are starting to get tired and grumpy) so they might be more receptive to trying new things at breakfast time.

Toast and cereal are both fine breakfasts (and there are a couple of recipes in this section for them) but it's good to think outside the box a bit and see breakfast as an opportunity to pack in the nutrients with fats, proteins, and veggies.

Most of the recipes in this chapter focuses on quick, nutritious food that you can make for the whole family. There are also various things that can be made in advance—especially helpful if your mornings are fraught with rushing to work, or dropping off older children at day care or school.

Because I'm still clinging onto the pre-baby days of relaxed weekend brunches, I've also included a couple of recipes that take a little bit more time to prepare for weekend breakfast feasts.

OATS THREE WAYS

Oats are versatile, easy to cook, and provide an excellent source of nutrition. They are high in soluble fiber, which makes them easy for babies to digest. They are also high in vitamin K and a good source of iron, magnesium (good for energy production and muscle function), and zinc (great for the immune system).

In these recipes I'm showing you three easy ways you can prepare oats to be suitable for your choice of weaning type, and at all stages of your baby's weaning journey.

OATMEAL

This is a simple basic oatmeal recipe, with options for loading with extra veggies and vitamins. One is a twist on my favorite cake, the other is rich in calcium (great for your baby's growing bones) and vitamin E (an antioxidant that supports the immune system and plays a role in cognitive development).

PREP: 5 minutes
COOK: 10 minutes
SERVES: 2 adults and 1 baby

*Using apple sauce (see page 160) will make a slightly sweeter dish, but grated apple is good, too.

** If peaches aren't in season then use pear. Canned peaches in juice are also fine!

CARROT CAKE OATS

1 cup (80 g) oats
1 cup (240 ml) milk of your choice
1 small carrot, peeled and finely grated
2 tbsp apple sauce (see page 160) or 1 apple, peeled and finely grated*
½ tsp pumpkin pie spice or cinnamon
1 tsp chopped walnuts (optional)

PEACH & ALMOND OATS

¾ cup (60 g) oats
1 cup (240 ml) milk of your choice
4 tbsp ground almonds
1 peach, peeled and finely chopped**
½ tsp cinnamon
1 tsp almond butter, to serve (optional)

Add all the ingredients to a saucepan and bring to a boil over medium heat. Reduce the heat and simmer for about 7 minutes, stirring continuously. If it's looking too thick, add a little water or extra milk as you cook. Leave to cool slightly before serving. If you are making the peach and almond oats, stir in the almond butter at the end.

OVERNIGHT OATS

Oats soaked in milk and yogurt go soft and creamy, and this is a lovely cold breakfast—perfect for summer.

PREP: 10 minutes + overnight in the fridge
SERVES: 1 adult and 1 baby

CARROT CAKE OVERNIGHT OATS

½ cup (40 g) oats

½ cup (120 ml) milk of your choice

4 tbsp natural yogurt

½ small carrot, peeled and finely grated

1 tbsp apple sauce (see page 160) or ½ apple, peeled and finely grated, plus more to serve

½ tsp pumpkin pie spice

PEACH & ALMOND OVERNIGHT OATS

6 tbsp oats

½ cup (120 ml) milk of your choice

4 tbsp natural yogurt

2 tbsp ground almonds, plus more to serve

1 peach, peeled and finely chopped, plus more to serve

½ tsp cinnamon

1 tsp almond butter, to serve (optional)

Mix all the ingredients together in a bowl. Decant into individual cups (or jars) and leave overnight in the fridge. Just before eating, sprinkle with some extra nuts, fruit, and nut butter, if you like.

OAT BITES

These baked oat bites are the perfect finger food.

PREP: 5 minutes
COOK: 15 minutes
(or 4 in a microwave)
MAKES: 4 baby servings

CARROT CAKE OAT BITES

½ cup (40 g) oats
6 tbsp milk
1 tbsp grated carrot
1 tbsp apple sauce (see page 160) or ½ apple, peeled and grated
½ tsp pumpkin pie spice or cinnamon

PEACH & ALMOND OAT BITES

6 tbsp oats
6 tbsp milk
2 tbsp ground almonds
¼ peach, peeled and finely chopped
½ tsp cinnamon

If you are using an oven preheat it to 350°F (180°C).

Mix together all the ingredients and then transfer to a small oven- or microwave-proof dish (about 5 × 5 in/13 × 13 cm). Bake in the oven for about 15 minutes or microwave at full power for 4 minutes.

Allow to cool before cutting into bite-sized pieces and then turn out of the dish. These will keep for 2 days in the fridge, and they freeze well.

GENERAL OATS TIP

If your baby isn't yet great with lumps you can use oat flour. Just whizz the oats in a blender until finely ground.

BREAKFAST SUSHI

Breakfast sushi is very much a sensory experience; the kids get to grab
the rolls, undo them, suck them, and practice their pincer grasp. Using a
buckwheat galette for the sushi adds an extra nutritional punch as buckwheat
is a plant-based source of complete protein. Bear in mind that the batter needs
time to rest, ideally overnight, so make the batter the night before.

TIME: 5 minutes
MAKES: 1 sushi roll

1 buckwheat galette or
  whole wheat wrap
1 tbsp nut or seed butter
  of your choice
1 banana, peeled
Small handful of berries
  to decorate (e.g.,
  raspberries, blueberries,
  or sliced strawberries)
1 tsp desiccated coconut
  or small seeds to
  decorate (sesame, chia,
  poppy, or hulled hemp
  all work well)

Spread one side of your galette or wrap with nut or seed butter. Place the banana at one end and roll it up in the galette or wrap.

Cut the roll into pieces about ¾ inch (2 cm) thick. Place onto a plate and put a berry on each slice. Sprinkle with coconut or seeds.

SUBSTITUTIONS

If your baby is struggling with slices of banana you can mash the banana and spread it on the wrap/galette with the nut butter. You can use yogurt instead of nut butter if your baby has an allergy.

TIP: You can use spare galettes for a quick lunch, too. Spread with cream cheese and/or mashed avocado and roll up, or roll up plain and use to scoop up dips.

BUCKWHEAT GALETTES

PREP: 5 minutes (plus
2 hours or overnight rest)
COOK: 20 minutes
MAKES: 6 galettes

4 tbsp buckwheat flour
4 tbsp whole wheat flour
1 cup (240 ml) milk of your
  choice
1 egg (or 1 chia egg, see
  page 182)
½ tsp coconut oil or butter

Put the flours, milk, and egg in a blender and blend until smooth. Leave the galette batter to rest in the fridge for a minimum of 2 hours, ideally overnight.

Heat the coconut oil or butter in a large nonstick pan over medium heat. Pour in about ⅙ of the batter and move the pan around so that the batter covers the base. Leave to cook for a couple of minutes until slightly golden at the edges, then flip and cook for about 1 minute on this side, then slide it onto a plate. Repeat until all the batter is used up. You probably don't need to add more oil or butter for each galette, but if they are starting to stick, then add a little more.

FREEZE: Place a piece of parchment paper between each to stop them from sticking together and so you can defrost individually.

RAINBOW PANCAKES

If you've had an unreasonably early wake-up, pour yourself a cup of coffee and bring a bit of fun to the table with these easy and bright pancakes.

These colorful banana pancakes are an ideal first food for babies as they are easy to hold and nice and soft for them to suck on and eat. Cooking the banana helps to produce a protein called amylase, which is needed to break down carbohydrates—babies don't produce as much amylase as adults so these pancakes are a great way to boost it.

PREP: 5 minutes
COOK: 15 minutes

Each recipe makes around 12 small pancakes and then you add the "colorings" from below. Double up and make as many as you would like!

Ideal first food (finger food)

BASE
2 eggs
1 banana
Coconut oil or butter, for cooking

FLOURS
Any of the following will work well as the "flour" in this recipe; mix and match to get lots of variety into your baby's breakfasts! Just use the amount in the color you are making.

- Oats or oat flour
- Whole wheat flour
- Spelt flour
- Buckwheat flour
- 1 tbsp coconut flour
- Desiccated coconut
- Ground almonds

OPTIONAL EXTRAS
½ tsp cinnamon
A few drops of vanilla extract or ½ tsp vanilla bean paste

YELLOW

2 tbsp peanut butter (or any other nut or seed butter)

2 tbsp flour

PINK

1 cooked and peeled beet

3 tbsp flour

BLUE

Handful of blueberries

4 tbsp flour

ORANGE

1 small carrot, peeled and grated

3 tbsp flour

GREEN

Handful of fresh spinach, chopped (or 2 tbsp frozen, defrosted)

3 tbsp flour

Heat a large nonstick pan over medium heat.

Mix together the eggs, banana, and your chosen flour and coloring/flavor in a blender (except for the blue pancakes where you stir the blueberries after blending).

Add a little coconut oil or butter to your pan. Pour in the batter to make small pancakes, no more than four in the pan at a time. The smaller they are the easier they are to flip (and are perfect for little hands!).

Let the pancakes cook for a couple of minutes. Look for small bubbles rising through the mix; this is a sign they are ready to flip. Flip the pancake and then cook for a minute or two more on the second side. Slide onto a plate and then cook the rest.

Serve the pancakes with more fruit, yogurt, mini seeds, crushed nuts, desiccated coconut, or nut butter.

TIP

These colorful pancakes freeze well and are great for your freezer stash. Instant breakfasts and snacks!

RAINBOW PANCAKES (pages 44–45)

VEGAN BAKED PANCAKE

PREP: 10 minutes
COOK: 30 minutes
SERVES: 2 adults and
2 children

Ideal first food (finger food)

1 cup (240 ml) plant-based
 milk

1½ tsp apple cider vinegar

1 tbsp ground flaxseed

1 cup (110 g) whole wheat
 flour

4 tbsp oats

1½ tsp baking powder

1½ tbsp coconut oil,
 melted, plus a bit more
 for cooking

1 cup or 3 handfuls of
 chopped fruit (e.g.,
 mango, kiwi, orange) or
 berries (e.g., blueberries,
 raspberries, strawberries)

Plant-based yogurt, to
 serve

This recipe originated from a waffle recipe by Isa Chandra Moskowitz (author of several amazing vegan recipe books). Over time I simplified it and adapted it for babies, and as a baked pancake it makes a lovely centerpiece for a weekend breakfast. You can still use this mix in a waffle iron if you have one (in fact, if you have a waffle iron please do it; the waffles are amazing!).

If you don't have a frying pan that you can put in the oven, you can use a cake pan instead. Alternatively, just make regular pancakes in a frying pan.

Preheat the oven to 400°F (200°C).

Mix together the milk, apple cider vinegar, and ground flaxseed. Whisk for about a minute until the milk has become frothy.

In another bowl, mix together the flour, oats, and baking powder.

Add the milk mixture, 4 tablespoons water, and the coconut oil to the flour mixture and mix well. Leave to stand for a few minutes to thicken.

In the meantime, heat up a 9-inch (23 cm) oven-proof frying pan over medium heat, and add a little coconut oil (if you are using a cake pan use the coconut oil to grease it). Once your pan has warmed up, and the oil has spread around, pour in the pancake mixture.

Scatter the fruit on to the top of the mix; there is no need to stir or push it in, and some bits will sink, which is fine!

Transfer the frying pan (or cake pan) to the preheated oven and cook for around 25 minutes until the top looks golden.

Cut into slices and enjoy with a dollop of yogurt.

COCONUT QUINOA BREAKFAST BOWL

PREP: 5 minutes
COOK: 25 minutes
SERVES: 2 adults and 1 baby

½ cup (90 g) quinoa
1 cup (240 ml) full-fat
  coconut milk
Handful of blueberries or
  raspberries
Handful of chopped
  mango, pineapple,
  papaya or kiwi
½ lime
2 tbsp mini seeds (e.g.,
  sesame, chia, and hulled
  hemp)
2 tbsp desiccated coconut

In our family, we call this summer porridge. The coconut taste and fresh, tropical fruit toppings make it feel lighter and more summery than regular porridge.

Quinoa is a complete protein (which means it contains all the amino acids your body needs) and also contains iron, so provides key nutrients for your growing baby. It's small, which makes it ideal for early spoon-fed weaning.

For baby-led weaning you can either serve this on loaded spoons for your baby to grab and feed themself, or you can cook the mix down to make it a little thicker, let it cool, and roll it into balls for your baby to pick up!

Rinse the quinoa by running it under the tap in a sieve. In a small pan add the quinoa, ¾ cup (180 ml) of the coconut milk and ½ cup (120 ml) water. Bring to a boil, then turn down the heat and gently simmer for about 20 minutes until the quinoa is cooked through. Stir occasionally to ensure the quinoa does not stick. When the quinoa is cooked turn off the heat and stir in the remaining coconut milk. Cover and set aside to cool a little.

In a bowl mix together the fruit. Zest the lime over the fruit and squeeze over the juice, too. Stir well.

Spoon the quinoa mix into three small bowls and top with the fruit. Sprinkle with the seeds and desiccated coconut.

NUT PUFFS

PREP: 5 minutes
COOK: 18 minutes
MAKES: about 20 baby portions

2 cups (40 g) buckwheat puffs
1 cup (30 g) brown rice puffs
1 cup (30 g) spelt puffs
½ cup (60 g) mixed small seeds (sesame, hulled hemp, chia, and/or poppy)
2 tsp cinnamon
2 tbsp coconut oil
3 tbsp cashew butter

SUBSTITUTIONS

To make a nut-free version you can replace the cashew butter with a mashed banana. If you want to omit the seeds, add half an extra cup of puffs instead.

I got this recipe from my good friend Lucy who was determined to recreate the '80s childhood magic of Sugar Puffs, which was a popular cereal in the UK, but without the sugar. I've further adapted Lucy's recipe to make it suitable for babies under 12 months, but if you want to add a little more sweetness for you, you can add two tablespoons of maple syrup to the nut and coconut oil mix.

If you can, use buckwheat puffs as they deliver an additional protein hit (they can sometimes be tricky to find in the stores). If you can't find any, increase the amounts of rice and spelt to make the total puff measurement 4 cups (100 g).

Preheat your oven to 320°F (160°C) and line a large baking sheet with parchment paper.

Add the puffs, seeds, and cinnamon to a bowl and mix well.

In a small pan gently melt the coconut oil and then add the cashew butter and stir until it's a smooth paste. Then pour over the puffs and stir well until each puff is lightly coated.

Pour into your baking sheet and spread out evenly. Place in the oven and bake for 15 minutes, stirring every 5 minutes. Remove from the oven and allow to cool completely.

The puffs are tasty on top of yogurt or a smoothie, with milk, or just on their own (they are great pincer grip practice!). If you are spoon-feeding, add milk and then leave it for a few minutes so the puffs become nice and soft.

Once you've made a batch it will keep in an airtight container for several weeks (although a batch has never lasted that long in our house!).

SMOOTHIES

SERVES: 2 babies

I love smoothies as they are a great way to use up any bits of fruit that may be past their prime. Some babies go off food when they are teething and just want drinks, so something like a smoothie is good to offer them. You can boost the nutrition (and color!) with some veggies, nuts, and oats, too.

Serve a smoothie in a bowl with extra toppings and it's a full sensory experience. This is one breakfast you will want your baby to be wearing a full bib (or be naked) for easy cleaning!

Blend the ingredients until smooth. Pour into a sippy cup or bowl and add any optional toppings.

Optional toppings
- Homemade cereal (see page 51)
- Small or milled seeds (e.g., sesame, poppy, chia, hulled hemp)
- Milled, ground, or finely chopped nuts
- Desiccated coconut
- Small berries (e.g., blueberry, pomegranate, raspberries)

THE GREEN ONE

1 banana

Handful of fresh or 2 tablespoons
    frozen spinach

½ tsp cinnamon

Small handful of oats

½ cup (120 ml) milk of your choice

THE PINK ONE

1 banana

2 handfuls of berries (e.g., raspberry or
    strawberry)

1 small cooked and peeled beet

Small handful of cashews or hulled hemp
    seeds

½ cup (120 ml) milk of your choice

THE ORANGE ONE

1 banana

1 small carrot, peeled and grated

1 orange, peeled and pith removed

1 tbsp desiccated coconut

½ cup (120 ml) milk of your choice

SMOOTHIES (page 52–53) & Nut puffs (page 51)

MINI EGG OR
TOFU FRITTATAS

PREP: 10 minutes
COOK: 20 minutes (egg frittatas), 30 minutes (tofu frittatas)
Each recipe makes 9 frittatas

Ideal first food (finger food)

FILLING
1 tsp olive oil
¼ red pepper, finely chopped
4 tbsp corn
3 white mushrooms, finely chopped
Small handful of grated cheese (optional)

EGG FRITTATAS
3 eggs
4 tbsp milk of your choice

TOFU FRITTATAS
1 block (10 ounces/280 g) extra firm tofu
½ cup (120 ml) milk of your choice
½ tsp ground turmeric
2 tbsp nutritional yeast

These mini frittatas have been a staple of ours since I started weaning my first child several years ago. Eggs are a brilliant source of nutrients for your growing baby. You can mix up the veggies depending on what you have to provide a range of colors, vitamins, and minerals.

The tofu version is very straightforward (but you'll need a blender) and is rich in protein and calcium. You could also add a few flakes of nutritional yeast, which is fortified with B12.

Preheat the oven to 350°F (180°C).

Heat the olive oil in a frying pan and gently fry all the chopped vegetables for about 5 minutes until cooked. Set aside.

EGG FRITTATA: Whisk together the egg and milk and then pour into 9 cups of a greased muffin pan, filling each cup halfway. Drop the vegetables in each cup and sprinkle with the cheese, if using. Bake for around 15 minutes until the mixture is set. Allow to cool slightly before turning out.

TOFU FRITTATA: Make the filling as above. Put all the remaining ingredients into a blender and blend until smooth. The mixture will be fairly thick (you want it so it drops easily off a spoon—if it's thicker than this add a little more milk).

Pour the mixture into 9 cups of a greased muffin pan, filling each cup halfway. Drop the vegetables in each cup, getting a nice mixture between each one. As the tofu mix is quite thick take a teaspoon and give each a quick stir so the vegetables don't just sit on top. Bake for about 25 minutes until the mixture is set. Allow to cool slightly before turning out.

Egg and tofu frittatas keep for 3 days in an airtight container in the fridge.

AVOCADO & TAHINI TOAST

Avocado toast needs no introduction and is an amazing first food for your baby. So why fix something that ain't broke? Well, I first had this avocado and tahini combo in a cafe in Sydney years ago and I was converted! The tahini makes the avocado extra creamy and it's incredibly delicious.

But it's not just the lovely taste—adding tahini to the avocado (already packed full of good fats and vitamins) is a great way of adding in some extra protein, calcium, and iron to your baby's diet.

Try to vary the bread you offer to your baby for the different nutrients and textures. I offer my children any bread I'd normally buy (which varies from sourdough, to whole wheat, to crusty white bread) with the crusts cut off. Toasting bread makes it easier for babies to eat as it doesn't go gluey when they suck on it (which can then get stuck on the roof of their mouth). Try and buy bread that hasn't been too processed—the fewer ingredients the better!

TIME: 5 minutes
SERVES: 1 adult and 1 baby

Ideal first food (finger food)

2 slices of bread
1 avocado
½ lime
1 tbsp tahini
Handful of sesame seeds
A few berries or
    pomegranate seeds
Salt and red pepper flakes,
    for adults (optional)

Toast your bread.

Meanwhile, scoop the insides out of the avocado, squeeze over the lime, add the tahini, and mash it using a fork. Spread on the toast. Sprinkle with some sesame seeds and berries, and for your piece, add a little salt and red pepper flakes if you like.

OTHER GREAT TOAST TOPPINGS

- Nut and seed butters topped with fresh berries or quick berry compote (see page 167)
- Unsalted butter sprinkled with a mix of small seeds such as chia, hulled hemp, sesame, or poppy
- Cream cheese and chia jam (see page 166)
- Nut butter with mashed banana

RASPBERRY & APPLE BREAKFAST MUFFINS

PREP: 10 minutes
COOK: 12–20 minutes
MAKES: 6–8 muffins or
20 mini muffins

Ideal first food (finger food)

¾ cup (80 g) whole wheat flour

¼ cup (20 g) oats, plus more to sprinkle on top

1 heaping tsp baking powder

1 eating apple, peeled and grated

¾ cup (80 g) fresh or ½ cup (60 g) frozen raspberries

1 egg (or 1 chia egg, see page 182)

¼ cup (60 ml) milk of your choice

1 tbsp tahini

2 tbsp coconut oil, melted, plus more to grease your muffin pan

Yogurt for dipping, optional

I love a breakfast muffin! You can make up a batch of these the day before and then have the easiest breakfast ever the next day. Excellent for rushed mornings.

The combination of raspberry and apple makes a perfect breakfast muffin. There is no added sugar but the raspberry and apple give it a lovely sweetness as well as keeping the muffins nice and moist (meaning fewer crumbs to clean up!). The tahini adds extra protein and calcium to the mix. All around a good start to the day!

Preheat the oven to 400°F (200°C). Lightly grease a muffin pan (8 large or 20 small cups) with coconut oil.

Mix together the flour, oats, and baking powder. Stir in the grated apple and raspberries. The muffins work better if the raspberries fall apart a bit so don't worry about being too gentle.

In another bowl whisk together the egg, milk, tahini, and coconut oil. Make a well in the flour and pour in the egg and milk mixture. Use a fork to mix it well.

Spoon the mixture into your muffin pan so that each cup is around two-thirds full. Sprinkle the extra oats on top of the muffins. Bake for around 18–20 minutes (12–15 minutes if you are making mini muffins) until the muffins are slightly golden on top and an inserted skewer comes out clean.

Remove from the oven and leave to cool for a few minutes before turning out onto a wire cooling rack and leaving to cool completely.

These will keep in an airtight container for 2–3 days, and they freeze really well (they are perfect for your freezer stash).

SUBSTITUTIONS

You can use any nut or seed butter in the place of tahini.
To make these seed-free replace the tahini with coconut oil.

SWEET POTATO ROSTI

PREP: 10 minutes
COOK: 20 minutes
MAKES: 9 rostis

Ideal first food (finger food)

1 sweet potato
  (about 7 ounces/200 g)
2 tbsp olive oil, plus extra
  for greasing, if needed
½ tsp garlic granules (or
  1 fresh clove, chopped)
2 tbsp whole wheat flour
1 egg, beaten (or 1 chia egg,
  see page 182)

On Saturday and Sunday we tend to opt for a slightly more substantial breakfast and enjoy not having to rush out of the door. These rostis are great served as part of a cooked breakfast topped with things like eggs, avocado, asparagus (when in season), and mushrooms. They are also perfect to go in your freezer stash—you can grab one out the night before and serve it to your baby for breakfast gently heated in the oven or microwave, or even cold if they prefer.

These rostis are baked, not fried, and cooking them in a muffin pan makes good individual portions and also helps the rostis retain their shape.

Preheat the oven to 400°F (200°C). Lightly grease a muffin pan (9 cups) with olive oil.

Grate the sweet potato (no need to peel it first) or use the medium grater blade of a food processor. Mix the grated sweet potato together with the remaining ingredients.

Spoon the mixture into the muffin pan and press down with a spoon so each rosti is about ½ inch (1 cm) thick.

Bake for about 20 minutes until the tops of the rostis are golden and crispy on top. Remove from the oven and leave to cool for a few minutes before gently turning out.

TIP: You can fry these, rather than bake, if you prefer (it's a little quicker). They will take about 5 minutes on each side over medium heat.

SUBSTITUTIONS

You can use a regular white potato instead of sweet potato if you like.

GREEN EGGS (OR TOFU) NO HAM

COOK: 5 minutes
SERVES: 1 baby or toddler

1 egg or ¼ block firm organic tofu (about 2½ ounces/75 g)
Handful of fresh spinach, finely chopped (or 2 tbsp frozen, defrosted)
1 tsp nutritional yeast (optional)
1 tsp butter or olive oil

A simple twist on regular scrambled eggs with a little nod to Dr. Seuss. I'm a big fan of getting lots of color into a baby's diet and these eggs are a super simple way to do that. Spinach leaves can be quite a tricky texture to eat without teeth so this is a great way to get your baby used to eating lots of green without having to navigate leaves.

For a complete breakfast serve alongside some toast and griddled mushrooms (or with a sweet potato rosti from page 64).

Put the egg or tofu and spinach in a blender and whizz together. Add the nutritional yeast, if using, and blend again.

Heat the butter or olive oil in a small frying pan. When the pan is hot add the mixture. Allow to cook for a couple of minutes, then stir gently to scramble. The spinach makes the egg mixture more watery so you'll need to cook it a bit more than regular scrambled egg. About 5 minutes of cooking is enough for the eggs and the tofu.

SUBSTITUTIONS

Any other greens, like kale, will also work instead of spinach (kale has a slightly stronger taste). Make sure you remove all the hard stems before using.

SWEET POTATO ROSTI (page 64) & GREEN EGGS (OR TOFU) NO HAM (page 65)

SNACKS & MINI MEALS

One of the consequences of having children is that as soon as my eldest hit 6 months old I became a slave to snacks. Leaving the house without a bag full of snacks is now as panic-inducing as realizing that I've left my wallet at home.

Because babies have such small stomachs, they get hungry often and quickly. It's totally normal to build in at least two official "snack times" to your day (mid-morning and mid-afternoon), and these will become even more important once your baby begins dropping milk feeds. Like most parents, I have found there are times when my children seem to enjoy snacks way more than actual meals. Rather than feel stressed about this, I've gotten into the habit of filling my bag with nutritious, veggie-loaded snacks and mini meals.

The snacks in this section are perfect for eating on the go—they are easy to transport and are not too messy (saving on stroller cleaning). Or you can serve them alongside some vegetable batons and/or a dip for a more substantial mini meal.

A little bit of time invested in prep goes a long way—half an hour spent cooking and you can have a freezer stash of healthy, filling snacks and mini meals that can last for two weeks. Grab a few bits every time you leave the house (which is a lot—babies can have hectic social lives!) and you know you always have something tasty and nutritious to offer.

BEET & CARROT FRITTERS WITH YOGURT & CUCUMBER DIP

Fritters are the perfect finger food for babies. The vegetables are grated so are easy to eat without teeth. You can make these with virtually any vegetables you have, but I love the vibrant pink of the beets in these. I like to make up a batch fresh for lunch and freeze the rest for on-the-go snacks.

The simple cucumber and yogurt dip is a great pairing for a light and delicious lunch and the yogurt adds a nice bit of extra calcium and fat—both essential for your growing baby.

PREP: 10 minutes
COOK: 30 minutes
MAKES: around
10–12 fritters

Ideal first food (finger food)

FRITTERS
1 carrot, peeled and grated
1 raw beet, peeled and grated
1 scallion, finely sliced (optional)
1 egg (or 1 chia egg, see page 182)
½ tsp ground cumin
2–3 tbsp whole wheat flour
1 tsp olive oil

YOGURT & CUCUMBER DIP
4 tbsp yogurt
¾-inch (2.5 cm) piece of cucumber, finely diced
1 tsp olive oil

Put the grated carrot and beet in a mixing bowl with the scallion (if using). Add the egg and cumin and mix well. Then add 2 tablespoons of the flour, and mix to make a batter-like texture. If the mixture seems too wet, add the extra tablespoon of flour.

Heat the olive oil in a large frying pan over medium heat. You can test if it's hot enough by adding a tiny bit of the batter—if it starts to cook immediately the oil is hot enough. Then add around 1 heaping tablespoon of batter for each fritter (I make about four at a time). Fry over low heat for about 5 minutes on each side.

Meanwhile, mix together all the ingredients for the dip. When all the fritters are cooked, serve with the dip.

The fritters will keep in the fridge for 2 days, and they freeze very well.

SUBSTITUTIONS

The fritters also go perfectly with a yogurt and tahini dip (see page 99) or hummus (see page 96), both of which are rich in calcium and healthy fats.

SWEET POTATO THINS

PREP: 15–25 minutes
COOK: 30 minutes
MAKES: about 24 thins

Ideal first food (finger food)

1 small sweet potato (about
    6 ounces/160 g), peeled
    and diced into ½-inch
    (1 cm) chunks
1¼ cups (100 g) oats
A few sprigs of rosemary
½ tsp baking powder
1 tbsp olive oil

VARIATION

With a simple ingredient switch you can make these into a healthy, sugar-free snack with hints of pumpkin pie. Perfect for the mid-afternoon slump (yours and your baby's!) just swap the rosemary for ½ teaspoon of pumpkin pie spice and the olive oil for a tablespoon of melted coconut oil.

This is a very simple, veggie-loaded cracker that you can pull together in a spare half-hour. For something so straightforward to make, these thins really pack in the nutrients. They are half oats and half sweet potato, which contains vitamin C and beta-carotene to support your baby's immune system, and both are a good source of fiber.

The dough is very easy to work with and my kids love helping to make them, both rolling out the dough and cutting it. Texture-wise they end up somewhere between a cookie and an oat cake—a crispy outside with a chewy center.

Preheat the oven to 350°F (180°C) and line a large baking sheet with parchment paper.

Steam (or boil) the sweet potato for about 10 minutes until it is soft. Then roughly mash it with a fork.

Put the oats in a blender with the rosemary and whizz until you have a fine flour texture.

Keep about a tablespoon of flour to one side for rolling. Add the rest of the oat flour, baking powder, and olive oil to a bowl along with the mashed sweet potato. Stir the mix until it becomes a dough. The easiest way to do this is to use your hands.

Dust your work surface with the reserved oat flour and roll the dough out to about ¼ inch (5 mm) thick. Use a 2-inch (5 cm) round cutter (or a glass if you don't have a cutter) to cut out about 24 circles. Reshape any extra bits and reroll as you need to, to use up all the dough. Put the circles on the lined baking sheet and bake for around 20 minutes until the thins start to become lightly golden and the edges crispy. Remove from the oven, transfer to a wire cooling rack, and leave to cool completely.

These will keep fresh in an airtight container for 3–4 days in the fridge and they freeze very well.

KALE, PEA & BUCKWHEAT PANCAKES

PREP: 10 minutes
COOK: 20 minutes
MAKES: 10 small pancakes

Ideal first food (finger food)

Handful of chopped kale
Handful of frozen peas, defrosted
2 eggs
3 tbsp buckwheat flour
1 tbsp natural (or plant-based) yogurt
½ tsp baking powder
½ tsp baking soda
Coconut oil or butter, for frying

Savory pancakes make an excellent on-the-go lunch or snack as they freeze well and don't make much of a mess when your baby is eating them.

Despite looking like a regular flour, buckwheat flour is a great option as it contains all nine of the essential amino acids that our bodies need (which means it's a complete protein), bumping up your baby's protein intake.

Lightly steam the kale for about 3 minutes until it is wilted. Add the steamed kale to a blender along with the peas, eggs, buckwheat flour, yogurt, baking powder, and baking soda. Blend until smooth.

Heat up some coconut oil or butter in a large frying pan over medium heat. Pour in the pancake batter to make small pancakes, about 2¾ inches (7 cm) in diameter. Cook for about 3 minutes until you see bubbles start coming through the mix to the top, then flip the pancakes and cook on the other side for another 2–3 minutes. Repeat with the rest of the batter to make about 10 pancakes.

Serve with a dip (see pages 96–103) and vegetable batons for a nutritious lunch.

These will keep in the fridge for a few days in an airtight container, and they freeze very well.

SUBSTITUTIONS

You can switch the kale for any leafy green such as spinach, chard, or broccoli.

PROTEIN-BOOSTED FRUIT & VEGGIES

Here are some ideas for serving fruit and vegetable snacks with a little extra protein and fat to support your growing baby's needs.

GET STUFFING!

FILL FRUITS AND VEGGIES WITH PROTEIN-PACKED FILLINGS

- Nut butters: peanut butter, cashew butter, pistachio butter (a nice pop of green!), almond butter
- Seed butters: pumpkin seed, tahini
- Yogurt: full-fat natural yogurt, coconut or soy yogurt

RASPBERRIES

(8 months+) Raspberries are perfect for stuffing. Use the handle of a teaspoon to get small scoops of filling and push them in.

CHERRY TOMATO

(8 months+) Cut in half and scoop out the seeds and pop in a filling such as cream cheese or mashed avocado. You can also use the fillings to the left.

CELERY STICKS

(Ideal first food) Celery is a natural filling boat. Slice into pieces no more than 4 inches (10 cm) long and fill. Your baby is unlikely to be able to eat the celery without teeth but will enjoy sucking out the fillings and will get some of the flavor of the celery. Cream cheese and mashed avocado are ideal fillings.

COAT YOUR FRUIT!

FRUITS TO COAT

- Banana
- Pineapple
- Kiwi
- Mango
- Melon

Some fruit can be quite tricky for a young baby to eat as it can be slippery. A coating makes it easier to grip.

COATINGS:

- Small seeds that can be left whole such as sesame, poppy, hulled hemp, and chia
- Milled nuts and seeds such as hazelnut, cashew, Brazil nut, walnut, and almond (ground almond is great too), and flax, pumpkin, and sunflower seeds
- Desiccated coconut, buckwheat, or quinoa puffed cereal milled to a dust

DO SOME DIPPING!

Dips aren't just for vegetables; fruit can benefit from a dip, too. Either serve the dip on the side or pre-dip the fruit for your baby.

Apples cut into thin rounds (I prefer rounds as slices can be a choking risk) and strawberries are ideal for dipping. Then dip into yogurt or crème fraîche, or nut and seed butters.

> **NOTE**
>
> Before using any nut or seed butters make sure you've followed the advice on page 29 about introducing your baby to allergenic foods.

PROTEIN-BOOSTED FRUIT & VEGGIES (pages 76–77)

CAULIFLOWER & BROCCOLI CHEESE MUFFINS

PREP: 10 minutes
COOK: 20 minutes
MAKES: about 12 muffins
or 20 mini muffins

Ideal first food (finger food)

1 cup (110 g) whole wheat
 flour
1½ tsp baking powder
1 cup (80 g) finely
 chopped broccoli
1 cup (80 g) finely
 chopped cauliflower
½ cup grated cheese or
 4 tbsp nutritional yeast
2 eggs (or 2 chia eggs, see
 page 182)
¼ cup (60 ml) milk of your
 choice
2 tbsp olive oil, plus extra
 for greasing

SUBSTITUTIONS

Pretty much any veg
can be finely chopped
or grated into a muffin.
Greens such as spinach
and kale should be
gently steamed first.

Savory muffins are one of my favorite weaning foods, and I like the nod to an oozy cauliflower and broccoli cheese gratin in these. You can whip up a batch fairly quickly, they freeze well, and are easy to transport and eat without being too messy (stroller snack goals!).

Cauliflower is also a bit of an unsung hero; despite looking pretty bland it packs a good nutritional punch and is particularly high in vitamins C and K and in folate, which support your baby's immune system and growth.

Preheat the oven to 350°F (180°C) and grease a 12-cup regular muffin pan or 20 cups of a mini muffin pan.

Mix together the flour, baking powder, broccoli, cauliflower, and cheese.

In a separate bowl whisk together the egg, milk, and olive oil. Add it to the flour and vegetable bowl and mix together thoroughly. If your mixture is looking very thick you can add a tablespoon or two more milk.

Spoon the mixture into the muffin pan, filling each cup about two-thirds full. Bake for about 20 minutes (or 15 minutes for mini muffins) until the muffins are golden on top and cooked through (test by inserting a skewer and if it comes out clean, they are ready).

Leave for a couple of minutes to cool and then turn out and leave on a wire cooling rack to cool.

The muffins will keep for around 3 days in an airtight container, and they freeze very well.

PUMPKIN, SPINACH & SEED MUFFINS

PREP: 10 minutes
COOK: 30 minutes
MAKES: 10 regular muffins
or 20 mini muffins

Ideal first food (finger food)

4 ounces (120 g) chopped peeled pumpkin, cut into ½-inch (1 cm) pieces

2 handfuls of fresh spinach, finely chopped (or 3 tbsp frozen, defrosted)

2 tbsp pumpkin seeds, chopped, plus extra to decorate

1 egg (or 1 flax egg, see page 182)

¼ cup (60 ml) milk of your choice

1 cup (110 g) whole wheat flour

1½ tsp baking powder

Olive oil, for greasing

SUBSTITUTIONS

Pumpkin can be replaced with butternut squash and the spinach with any leafy greens.

A muffin containing some of my favorite nutritious foods, and they taste delicious, too. The pumpkin keeps these muffins nice and moist and the pumpkin seeds add a great dose of essential fats and zinc, which are great for your baby's brain and cognitive development. Spinach is a nutritional powerhouse delivering iron and calcium, which are all vital for your growing baby. An all-around excellent muffin!

These muffins are great with soup or a dip for a light lunch, or pop a couple in your diaper bag for snacks when out and about.

Preheat the oven to 350°F (180°C) and lightly oil 10 cups of a regular muffin pan or 20 cups of a mini muffin pan.

Steam (or boil) the pumpkin for about 10 minutes until it is very soft. If you are using fresh spinach, put it in a sieve over the sink and then pour boiling water over it to wilt slightly.

Mix together the cooked pumpkin, spinach, and pumpkin seeds. In another bowl, whisk together the egg and milk. Add the flour and baking powder to the milk and egg mixture and stir to combine.

Add the pumpkin, spinach, and pumpkin seed mixture and mix gently. Spoon the mixture into the muffin pan and sprinkle with extra pumpkin seeds. Bake for around 20 minutes (or 15 minutes for mini muffins) until the muffins are golden on top and cooked through (test by inserting a skewer and if it comes out clean, they are ready).

Leave to cool for a couple of minutes in the pan and then turn out on a wire cooling rack to cool fully. These will keep in an airtight container for 2–3 days, or pop them in the freezer (if you take them out in the morning they'll be defrosted by lunch).

CAULIFLOWER & BROCCOLI CHEESE MUFFINS (page 80)
PUMPKIN, SPINACH & SEED MUFFINS (page 81)

SAVORY OAT BAR

These oat bars are a total throwback to the vegetarian food of the '70s and '80s—nutritious, simple, and filling. Packed with oats, seeds, and vegetables, they are rich in protein, healthy fats, and fiber. My kids always linger by the oven when I'm cooking these waiting for first dibs on a piece.

They are very easy to make (perfect for nap-time baking) and a great way to boost your freezer stash.

PREP: 10 minutes
COOK: 30 minutes
MAKES: around 16–20 oat bars

Ideal first food (finger food)

4 tbsp pumpkin seeds
4 tbsp sunflower seeds
1 cup (80 g) oats
1 carrot, peeled and grated
½ zucchini, grated
1 cup (120 g) grated cheese (or 4 tbsp nutritional yeast)
2 eggs
4 tbsp olive oil

Preheat the oven to 350°F (180°C) and line an 8-inch (20 cm) square baking pan with parchment paper.

Chop the pumpkin and sunflower seeds in a blender until a fine crumble. You can leave them whole for older children, if you like.

Mix together the oats, carrot, zucchini, seeds, and cheese. In another bowl, beat the eggs and then pour into the mix. Add the olive oil and stir well.

Pour the mixture into the baking pan and press it down so it's firmly packed. Bake for around 30 minutes until the mixture is set and golden. Remove from the oven. Let it cool for a few minutes and then use a knife to cut it into 16–20 portions. Leave to cool completely before removing from the pan.

Enjoy as a snack, or with soup for a more substantial lunch.

These will keep for 2–3 days in an airtight container, and they freeze well.

UPGRADES & SUBSTITUTIONS

You could add fresh, chopped herbs, and different veggies. I like cauliflower (about 6 florets, finely chopped); or for a Mediterranean twist how about a red pepper (finely chopped), half a cup of corn kernels and a little chopped oregano.

For a seed-free version that still packs in the extra protein, replace the seeds with half a cup of flaked quinoa.

POLENTA FRIES

PREP: 5 minutes
COOK: 35 minutes
MAKES: about 18 chips

Ideal first food (finger food)

½ cup (80 g) instant polenta
1½ cups (350 ml) low-salt stock
1 tbsp olive oil, plus extra for greasing

My babies have all been dip obsessed. We would get through loads of toast and breadsticks so a lot of my weaning recipes are the result of trying to break up the bread monopoly. These simple polenta fries are a great (and naturally gluten-free) alternative to toast. Polenta is a great complex carbohydrate, which means it will provide your baby with a steady release of energy.

Preheat the oven to 400°F (200°C). You need two baking pans; one to spread the mixture onto, and another to cook the fries on. Oil 1 of the pans.

Put the polenta and stock into a saucepan and bring to a boil. Reduce the heat and simmer for around 3 minutes until the mixture is thick.

Spread the polenta in the unoiled baking pan to about ½ inch (1 cm) thick. Once the polenta is cool, slice into about 18 sticks with a sharp knife. Carefully place them on the oiled baking pan.

Drizzle with the oil and bake in the oven for around 25–30 minutes until golden and crisp.

Best served with a killer dip; hummus is always popular in our house (see page 96).

OPTIONAL EXTRA FLAVORINGS

If you fancy adding some extra flavor to these fries, add one of the following to the pan along with the polenta when you start cooking: 2 tablespoons of nutritional yeast, a handful of grated cheese, a teaspoon of dried oregano or rosemary, or a handful of grated carrot.

CHICKPEA CRACKERS

PREP: 5 minutes
COOK: 15 minutes
MAKES: about 24 crackers

Ideal first food (finger food)

2¼ cups (225 g) chickpea flour, plus extra for dusting

4 tbsp small seeds (e.g., sesame, chia, hulled hemp, or poppy)

1 tsp baking powder

½ cup (60 g) finely grated cheese (or 4 tbsp nutritional yeast)

4 tbsp olive oil, plus extra for brushing

NOTE

If you make this with nutritional yeast instead of cheese, you might like to add a little more olive oil to the dough to help it come together.

This is a recipe I always come back to as it's a perfect snack or great with dips for lunch. The chickpea flour means these crackers are rich in protein and a good source of iron, as well as being naturally gluten-free. They are also excellent for teething babies to gum on.

If you don't have chickpea flour, this recipe also works with whole wheat flour, which is a good source of fiber, iron and zinc. Chickpea flour makes the dough slightly harder to work with than regular flour as it can be quite sticky, so if you are making these with older children you might want to use half chickpea flour and half whole wheat flour so the cutting out is easier!

Preheat the oven to 375°F (190°C) and line a large baking sheet with parchment paper.

Mix together the chickpea flour, seeds, baking powder, and grated cheese. Add the olive oil and mix well (the mix will be quite crumbly). Then add water a tablespoon at a time until dough comes together.

Roll out the dough on a floured surface to about ¼ inch (5 mm) thick. Using a 2-inch (5 cm) round cutter (or a glass if you don't have a cutter) cut out about 24 crackers and put on the lined baking sheet. Reshape any extra bits and reroll as you need to, to use up all the dough. Brush each cracker with a little olive oil.

Bake for 12–15 minutes until golden. Remove from the oven, transfer to a wire cooling rack, and leave to cool completely. These will keep in an airtight container for about a week.

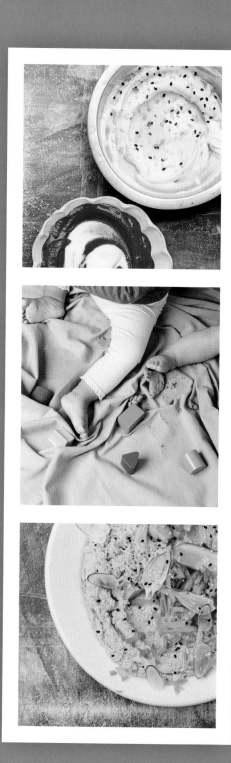

DIPS & STAPLE SAUCES

Dips and sauces are ideal weaning foods; they are great if you are doing baby-led weaning as babies are generally naturally inquisitive about dipping batons of food (or their fingers) into something soft (no guarantee it'll make it to their mouth though . . .). For spoon-weaning, dips and sauces are perfect "normal food" purées; food that your children will eat as they get older, rather than only as baby food.

Contrary to how messy they sound, dips are also great in a packed lunch, along with some Chickpea Crackers (see page 91), Sweet Potato Thins (see page 72), and vegetable batons, or in a good old sandwich. Put some in a reusable pouch that you can squeeze onto a cracker or a spoon, or get a bento box with a good seal.

I've included my staple sauces in this chapter, which are the ones I always rely on and that always get eaten. Stirred into pasta or rice, or with baked potatoes they make the quickest, easiest meals. I keep a supply in my freezer and they can be spread on pizza bases, or made into pies and tarts—yummy and versatile!

NOTE: Garlic for babies
A lot of the no-cook dips in this section use garlic powder or granules rather than fresh garlic. This is because I've found it less overpowering for young children (babies have much more sensitive palates than adults). If you don't have any just use a little fresh garlic; you will need to crush and chop it and gently cook it in a little olive oil first. Or just leave it out!

PESTO BUILDER

It's no secret that kids love pesto pasta, but the store-bought jars contain a lot of salt. But if you make it yourself (minus the salt!) it's a great sauce for kids: This one is full of veggies and contains good fats and protein, too.

Pesto is a good way to get babies to eat kale or spinach. This builder will help you get creative with lots of different pestos. Feel free to combine your vegetables (I like 50/50 kale and spinach) and mix up your nuts and seeds depending on what you have in the cupboard.

A batch of pesto has many uses. Obviously perfect with pasta, it can also be mixed into muffins or omelettes, or used in any of the quick hack meals (see pages 136–137 and 148–149).

SERVES: 2 adults and 2 children. Makes 8 baby portions

Juice of ½ lemon
1 tsp garlic powder or granules
Big glug of olive oil (enough to get your blender going)

Steam the spinach or kale for about 3 minutes until wilted.

Toast the nuts and/or seeds for about 2 minutes in a nonstick frying pan until they have a little color on all sides (there is no need to use any oil).

Blend together the vegetable, nuts, flavoring, lemon juice, garlic, and olive oil to get the consistency of pesto. For a baby I would recommend a smooth texture so that you don't risk there being larger pieces of nuts and/or seeds. Add a little water if you need to make the mix smoother. If the pesto tastes a little bitter add some lemon juice.

CHOOSE YOUR VEGETABLE:

- Large handful of fresh spinach (or 3 tbsp frozen, defrosted)
- Large handful of kale
- Large handful of basil
- 2 roasted peppers
- 1 cup (140 g) frozen peas, defrosted
- ½ head broccoli, cooked
- 1 cup (100 g) sun-dried tomatoes
- 2 cooked and peeled beets

CHOOSE YOUR SEEDS OR NUTS:

- Handful of pine nuts
- Handful of cashews
- Handful of walnuts
- Handful of sunflower seeds
- Handful of pumpkin seeds

Nut- and seed-free version:
½ avocado

CHOOSE YOUR FLAVORINGS:

- Handful of grated cheese
- 2–3 tbsp nutritional yeast
- Lemon juice, to taste (optional)

TIP

Spoon into an ice cube tray and freeze individual portions.

BASIC HUMMUS

SERVES: 2 adults and
2 children. Makes 8 baby
portions

One 15.5-ounce (400 g)
   can chickpeas, drained
   and rinsed
1½ tbsp tahini
½ tsp garlic granules or
   powder
2 tbsp olive oil
Juice of about ½ lemon
6 tbsp water

This wouldn't be a vegetarian cookbook without hummus!
Like store-bought pesto, you'll find store-bought hummus
tends to be quite high in salt, which means it's not great for
weaning babies. So get into the habit of making it yourself
(it really doesn't take long at all, especially using canned
chickpeas) and you can get all the benefits of chickpeas
and tahini (between them they are packed with protein,
iron, calcium, and essential fats), without the added salt.
The lemon juice also gives a hit of vitamin C.

Blend all the ingredients until you get your desired
consistency. Add a little more water if the hummus is still a
bit thick. Taste, and add more lemon juice if you like. This
keeps for 2–3 days in the fridge.

TIP

You can also freeze
hummus; just spoon
into an ice cube tray for
individual baby portions.

CARROT, BEET, OR RED PEPPER HUMMUS

SERVES: 2 adults and 2 children. Makes 8 baby portions

2 carrots, 2 beets, or 1 red pepper

2 tbsp olive oil, plus extra for roasting

One 15.5-ounce (400 g) can chickpeas, drained and rinsed

1½ tbsp tahini

½ tsp garlic granules or powder

Juice of ½ lemon

½ tsp ground cumin (optional)

For extra color and flavor, you can also add roast vegetables to your hummus. If your baby has struggled with the taste of regular hummus give these ones a try as the vegetables sweeten it slightly.

Preheat the oven to 350°F (180°C).

Wash the carrots or beets (no need to peel them) if using, and then cut the carrots, beets, or pepper into quarters. Drizzle with a little olive oil and roast for about 30 minutes until soft.

Then add all the ingredients and 3 tablespoons water to a food processor or blender and blend. Add another 3 tablespoons water slowly until the hummus is the desired consistency.

SUBSTITUTIONS

You can use those little packs of cooked beets that you get in the supermarket or fresh beets for this recipe. You don't have to roast the precooked beets, unless you want to.

Hummus does not need to be made out of chickpeas. Other beans work just as well so experiment! Butterbeans, cannellini beans, navy beans, and mung beans all work well. The only difference is other beans may have a slightly higher moisture content so add the water gradually to ensure your hummus doesn't end up too runny.

If your baby has a sesame allergy just leave the tahini out and add the water gradually until it's the right consistency.

FAVA DIP

PREP: 5 minutes (plus 30 minutes soaking)
COOK: 40 minutes
SERVES: 2 adults and 2 children. Makes 8 baby portions

½ cup (90 g) yellow split peas
4 tsp olive oil
½ onion, finely diced

Confusingly this is made with yellow split peas rather than fava beans, but it is known by this name all across the world. This dip is Greek and when my friend Stella introduced it to me in Athens I was an instant convert. It does have a fairly long cooking time, but it only contains three ingredients and it's very low maintenance (the instructions are strictly not to stir while the peas are cooking!).

High in protein and iron, this is a brilliant alternative to hummus especially if your baby has a sesame allergy. Serve with some vegetable batons to get the most out of the iron in the split peas.

Cover the peas with water and soak them for at least half an hour.

Add 2 teaspoons of the olive oil to a saucepan over medium heat. Cook the onion for about 10 minutes until softened.

Drain and rinse the split peas and then add them to the onions. Add 2 cups (500 ml) water and bring to a boil. Once boiling turn the heat down so it is gently simmering. Spoon off any of the scum that rises to the top, and then cover and leave to simmer, without stirring, for about half an hour, until the split peas are cooked (add more water if it's looking dry before the peas are cooked). Remove from the heat and leave to cool for 15 minutes.

Transfer the peas to a blender and add the remaining olive oil. Blend until smooth.

This keeps for 2–3 days in the fridge. You can also freeze; just spoon into an ice cube tray for individual baby portions.

VEGGIE FROM THE START

YOGURT DIPS

If your baby is going through a yogurt phase (lots of parents find their babies only want yogurt when teething), here are a few nutrition-loaded dips you can make with it. You can make these with a plant-based yogurt, however you'll need to take care to choose one that tastes like plain natural yogurt and doesn't have added sugar—there are some soy varieties that should fit the bill.

TAHINI DIP

PREP: 5 minutes
MAKES: 4 baby portions

3 tbsp natural yogurt
1 tbsp tahini
½ tsp garlic granules or powder
Generous squeeze of lemon juice
½ tsp olive oil

A great dip packed with healthy fats, protein, and calcium, which are all excellent for your growing baby. This dip is incredibly versatile and goes with many different foods: veggie batons, fritters, crackers, on baked potatoes, with a Buddha Bowl (see pages 109–119), and so on.

Put all the ingredients in a bowl and mix together. Taste, and add more lemon juice and garlic powder if you'd like.

SUBSTITUTIONS

You can turn this into a dairy-free dip quite easily by using soy yogurt or just replacing the yogurt with 1 extra tablespoon of tahini. You will need to add 2 tablespoons water, stirring slowly as you add it, and add a little extra lemon juice, to taste.

From top left: FAVA DIP (p. 98), ROAST BEET DIP (p. 102), TAHINI DIP (p. 99), EDAMAME HUMMUS (p. 114), BEET HUMMUS (p. 97), RED PEPPER HUMMUS (p. 97), EGGPLANT DIP (p. 103), BASIC HUMMUS (p. 96)

ROAST BEET DIP

PREP: 5 minutes
COOK: 30 minutes
MAKES: 4 baby portions

2 beets
Olive oil, for roasting
½ tsp ground cumin
½ tsp garlic granules or
  powder
4–5 tbsp natural yogurt

The color of this dip is amazing! However, you might want to make sure your baby has a decent bib for this one—beets aren't known for being forgiving on your laundry. . . . The pigments that give beets their bright, deep colors (called betalains) have antioxidant properties—great for the immune system and with benefits for eye health, too (so worth that extra laundry!).

You can use either precooked beets or roast them from scratch; both will taste great.

Preheat the oven to 350°F (180°C). Peel and quarter the beets, place them on a baking pan, drizzle with a little olive oil and roast for 30 minutes. Leave to cool.

Put the beets in a blender. Add the cumin and garlic. The amount of yogurt needed to get a nice thick dip consistency will depend on how much water is in your cooked beets; start by adding 2 tablespoons and then blend until the dip is combined. Add the rest of the yogurt 1 tablespoon at a time and mix by hand until the dip is the desired consistency.

EGGPLANT DIP

PREP: 5 minutes
COOK: 1–1 ½ hours
MAKES: 4 baby portions

1 eggplant
½ tsp garlic granules or
　powder
1 tsp olive oil
2–4 tbsp natural yogurt

This is another one of my friend Stella's amazing Greek recipes. It's her mom's recipe with the salt taken out, and is great for kids, especially yogurt-obsessed ones!

Preheat the oven to 400°F (200°C).

Pierce the skin of the eggplant a couple of times with a sharp knife or fork. Place the whole thing on a baking pan and roast for around 1–1½ hours until the middle is soft and the skin is charred. Set aside to cool.

Once the eggplant is cool scoop out the insides and put in a bowl. Add the garlic granules or powder and olive oil and mash with a fork until smooth. Add the yogurt a tablespoon at a time and mix well until the dip is the desired consistency. You can use a blender if you want the dip to be completely smooth.

CHEEZE SAUCE

PREP: 5 minutes
COOK: 5 minutes
SERVES: 4 children

1 small potato, peeled and
  diced
1 carrot, peeled and diced
A couple of cauliflower
  florets, chopped
Handful of grated cheese
1–2 tbsp nutritional yeast
  (optional)

This sauce is easier to make than a regular béchamel (no stirring) and you can cook it in the time it takes to cook some pasta to go with it! The base is vegetables—while I'm not big into "sneaking" vegetables into your baby's diet, if the vegetable provides a shortcut (and a wonderful "plastic cheese" orange coloring) then who am I to complain?!

I suggest serving this alongside a few steamed batons of carrot and cauliflower to have a variety of textures for your baby to pick up and explore.

Steam or boil the potato, carrot, and cauliflower for about 5 minutes until softened. Let the veggies cool slightly (or run under cold water) and then put them in a blender along with the other ingredients. Blend until smooth. You might need to add 1 or 2 tablespoons water if the mix is looking too thick.

This freezes well. I'd recommend making up a double batch and then freezing some individual portions for quick dinners.

SUBSTITUTIONS

You can replace the vegetables with any other orange or yellow vegetables you have on hand, e.g., pumpkin, butternut squash, or corn.

To make this dairy-free replace the cheese with a handful of soaked cashew nuts. Soaking cashews in boiling water for 30 minutes will make them softer and easier to blend.

VEGGIE-LOADED TOMATO SAUCE

PREP: 10 minutes
COOK: 30 minutes
SERVES: 2 adults and
2 children

1 tbsp olive oil
½ onion, peeled and diced
2 cloves garlic, peeled and
   chopped
1 stick celery, finely
   chopped
1 carrot, peeled and grated
½ zucchini, grated
1 red pepper, finely
   chopped
Two 14.5-ounce cans
   chopped tomatoes
1 tsp dried oregano (or a
   few sprigs of fresh)
1 tsp balsamic vinegar

In this sauce I use carrot, zucchini, and red pepper to sweeten the tomatoes and to provide an extra nutritional hit. Any similar vegetables will work well, too, such as pumpkin, squash, sweet potato, etc. Feel free to add any more vegetables that you like, such as yellow peppers, eggplant, mushrooms, and so on.

Heat the olive oil in a frying pan over medium heat and add the onion. Cook for around 10 minutes until soft. Add the garlic and cook for 1 minute more.

Add the celery, carrot, zucchini, and red pepper (and any other veggies you like) and cook for a few more minutes. Add the chopped tomatoes, oregano, balsamic vinegar, and about ½ cup (120 ml) water. Stir well and then simmer gently for around 20 minutes until it's reduced and all the veggies are cooked through.

Remove from the heat and leave to cool. Transfer to a blender or food processor (you might need to do this in batches) and blend until smooth.

This freezes incredibly well. Freeze any leftovers in individual portions using an ice cube tray.

BOLOGNESE TWIST

Add a can of cooked lentils (any kind you like) when you add the chopped tomatoes and this becomes a veggie-loaded lentil "Bolognese" sauce. You can either blend it smooth or leave it slightly chunky to add a bit of texture (I often blend half and leave half). Serve with pasta or as a quick filling for pastry parcels (see page 137).

VEGGIE-LOADED TOMATO SAUCE (page 105) & CHEEZE SAUCE (page 104)

BABY BUDDHA BOWLS

Buddha Bowls is essentially a jazzed-up name for a snacky plate with lots of tempting bits and pieces of food all served in a bowl. The different foods are kept separate and the emphasis is on bright and simple—perfect for baby's exploration and easy to prepare for you.

As babies develop it's normal for them to enter phases of fussiness when it comes to food. Keeping components separate is an easy way to stop mealtimes from disintegrating when they are going through phases of rejecting food. Don't stress about them trying everything—your job is to offer lots of nutritious foods and they get to choose what they want to eat.

Buddha Bowls are perfect for sharing with your baby at home, or you can put it all in a bento box for when you're out for the day. Make another bowl for yourself, and add a zingy dressing or some chile to your portion.

BUILDING YOUR BUDDHA BOWL

The components of a Buddha Bowl are: a grain (or carbohydrate), a protein, and a selection of vegetables. Basically, a really balanced meal! Each of these will make enough for one adult and one small person. Just choose at least one of each from the following lists:

1. CHOOSE A GRAIN

Handful of cooked quinoa, couscous, brown rice, cracked bulgur wheat, barley, buckwheat, pasta, or noodles

2. GO CRAZY WITH THE VEGGIES

Add three or four different types of vegetables. You don't need to cook them in a fancy way—just prepare them in a way that is suitable for your baby's weaning stage.

Steamed or roasted batons such as carrot are good for all babies (you can leave whole or mash lightly).

Grated veggies such as zucchini and carrot are a nice texture change, and good for babies whose pincer grasps are more developed.

Small veggies like peas and corn are great for texture and for working on pincer grip.

Raw and sliced veggies such as cucumbers, tomatoes, and avocados work well, too. Leave the skin on avocado batons for younger babies—it makes them easier to pick up and stops them from becoming mushy.

3. ADD A PROTEIN

Boiled egg, slices of tofu, handful of cheese, or legumes (e.g., lentils, navy beans, or black beans. Mash or purée the beans if you like.)

Any of the dips in the dip section (see pages 96–103) work well in a Buddha Bowl.

4. ADD SOME SPRINKLES

About a tablespoon of:

Whole mini seeds such as poppy, hulled hemp, chia, and sesame seeds

Ground-up whole seeds such as pumpkin and sunflower seeds

Ground-up nuts such as cashews, peanuts, and walnuts

5. ADD SOME ZING

For your bowl, and as your child gets older, add some extra flavor with black pepper, salt, grated fresh ginger, chopped fresh chile or red pepper flakes, salad dressing, a squeeze of lemon or lime.

SATAY BOWL

8+

PREP: 10 minutes (plus
2 hours if marinating the
tofu, optional)
COOK: 20 minutes
SERVES: 1 adult and 1 baby

½ block (140 g) extra firm
   organic tofu, cut into
   ½ × 4-inch (1 × 10 cm)
   batons

One 2-ounce (50g) nest
   whole wheat noodles

¼ head broccoli, cut into
   small florets

2 tbsp toasted sesame oil
   (optional)

½ cucumber, grated

1 carrot, grated

Handful of lettuce leaves

2 tsp sesame seeds to
   garnish (optional)

1 tsp soy sauce or tamari,
   for the adult portion

SATAY DIPPING SAUCE

4 tbsp peanut butter
   (crunchy or smooth)

4 tbsp coconut milk (if it
   has separated make sure
   you have an equal mix of
   the fatty part and liquid
   part)

½ tsp lemon juice

½ tsp garlic granules or
   powder

2 tbsp water

The satay dipping sauce with this bowl is delicious. It's incredibly addictive and lifts what is quite a bland ingredient (the tofu) to heavenly status. This is a baby-friendly satay sauce with no added soy sauce and uses coconut milk, rather than sugar or syrup, as a sweetener.

This recipe uses grated cucumber and carrot, but if you are baby-led weaning and your baby hasn't developed their pincer grasp you can leave the cucumber in batons and steam the carrot. I've included lettuce leaves, which are lovely in this bowl; your baby might struggle to eat leaves at the moment but it's nice for them to explore the texture and to try picking them up and sucking.

If you want, marinate the tofu using the salt-free and baby-friendly marinade on page 133. Put the tofu batons in a bowl and pour the marinade over. Leave for a minimum of 2 hours.

Cook the noodles according to the package instructions and set aside. Meanwhile, steam the broccoli for 4–5 minutes until it is cooked. Set aside to cool.

To make the satay sauce put all the ingredients for the sauce into a blender and pulse until everything is mixed.

If you haven't marinated the tofu put it in a bowl and add the toasted sesame oil, and stir carefully, making sure each piece of tofu is coated.

Heat a frying pan over medium heat, then add the tofu and cook for a few minutes on each side until it is golden and starting to crisp (you don't want it to be too crunchy otherwise your baby will struggle to eat it).

Arrange the noodles, tofu, and vegetables in a bowl and pour the satay sauce over or keep on the side for dipping. Sprinkle on the seeds, if using. Add soy sauce or tamari to your portion, if you like.

SUSHI BOWL

PREP: 10 minutes
COOK: 25 minutes
SERVES: 1 adult and 1 baby

¼ cup (40 g) brown rice

1 carrot, grated or cut into batons

½ cucumber, cut into batons

1 avocado, diced (leave the skin on to help early weaners, or mash)

4 radishes, thinly sliced

1 tsp seaweed sprinkles (optional)

2 tsp sesame seeds (optional)

EDAMAME HUMMUS

1 cup (125 g) frozen, shelled edamame beans

1 tbsp tahini

1½ tbsp lemon juice

¼ tsp garlic granules or powder

4 tbsp water

OPTIONAL DRESSING FOR ADULTS

1 tbsp tamari or soy sauce

1 tsp sesame oil

½-inch (1 cm) piece fresh ginger, grated

Juice of ½ lemon

½ clove garlic, crushed

Dash of maple syrup

Edamame beans are a great source of protein, calcium, and vitamin C so ideal for your growing baby. The shape of edamame can be a little tricky for babies until they master their pincer grasp (and get a few teeth) so this hummus is a perfect solution. I buy bags of frozen shelled edamame, which work great for this recipe.

For even more of a sushi kick, top the sushi bowl with a few seaweed sprinkles. Seaweed contains lots of minerals so a little bit is fine for a baby occasionally.

Cook the rice according to the package instructions.

Meanwhile, steam the carrot batons if you need to, for 3 minutes, until soft.

Cook the edamame beans for the hummus in boiling water for about 4 minutes. Put all the edamame hummus ingredients in a blender and blend until smooth.

In two bowls (one for you, one for baby), arrange the rice, veggies, and a generous serving of the edamame hummus. Sprinkle with the seaweed and/or sesame seeds, if using.

To make the dressing, put all the dressing ingredients in a small glass and mix well. Pour over your portion.

Any leftover hummus will keep for a few days in the fridge and is great for dipping or as a sandwich filling.

DUKKAH BOWL

PREP: 15 minutes
COOK: 30 minutes
SERVES: 1 adult and 1 baby

½ red pepper, chopped

¼ eggplant, chopped

½ zucchini, chopped

1 tbsp olive oil, plus more for serving

5 tbsp cracked bulgur wheat

2 eggs

1 tbsp hummus (see page 96)

1 tsp balsamic vinegar, for adult portion

DUKKAH

2 tbsp hazelnuts

1 tsp cumin seeds

1 tsp coriander seeds

2 tsp sesame seeds

Dukkah sounds quite fancy but it's really just a ground-up spice and nut mix that really adds flavor and nutrients to this bowl. It provides a protein and healthy fat boost and is a gentle introduction to spices for your baby. If you buy preroasted unsalted nuts it's even quicker to make.

Dukkah and boiled egg are a great combination, but if you have any hummus made up then this is also a great addition to the bowl (see pages 96, 97, or 114).

If you want the vegetables to be finger food for your baby, chop them into batons. Alternatively you can chop them smaller and mash them after cooking for spoon-feeding.

Preheat the oven to 350°F (180°C). Put the pepper, eggplant, and zucchini on a baking pan and drizzle with a little olive oil. Bake for about 20 minutes until they are cooked through and soft.

Meanwhile, to make the dukkah, heat a frying pan or saucepan over medium heat. Add the hazelnuts and gently toast them in the pan, stirring occasionally for about 5 minutes, and then add the seeds and toast for about 3 minutes (be careful not to let them burn). Once they are all toasted let them cool. Mill the mixture in a blender.

Cook the bulgur wheat according to the instructions on the package.

Bring a medium pan of water to a boil. Gently lower the eggs into the water and cook for 10 minutes until hard-boiled. Rinse with cold water and then peel. Cut in half.

Assemble the bowls with the bulgur wheat, roasted veggies, egg halves, and hummus. Drizzle with a little oil (and balsamic vinegar for the adult portion) and sprinkle with the dukkah.

MEXICAN BOWL

8+

PREP: 15 minutes
COOK: 25 minutes
SERVES: 1 adult and 1 baby

1 sweet potato, peeled and chopped into cubes or batons

1 tbsp olive oil

5 tbsp quinoa

Half a 15.5-ounce (440 g) can cooked black or kidney beans, drained and rinsed

½ cucumber, cut into batons

½ cup (70 g) corn kernels (canned, drained, or frozen, defrosted if needed)

Juice of ½ lime

Small handful of cilantro, roughly chopped

OPTIONAL TOPPINGS FOR ADULT PORTION

Small fresh chile, chopped, and salt

GUACAMOLE

1 avocado

¼ tsp garlic granules or powder

Juice of ½ lime

3 cherry tomatoes, finely chopped

Few sprigs of cilantro, finely chopped

Black beans and guacamole are a delicious combination in this easy and quick Buddha Bowl. If your baby has mastered their pincer grasp you can leave the beans whole, otherwise gently mash them first.

Preheat the oven to 400°F (200°C). Put the sweet potatoes on a baking pan, drizzle with the olive oil, and roast for 25 minutes until they are cooked through.

Meanwhile, cook the quinoa according to the package instructions and then set aside.

To make the guacamole, mash the avocado with the garlic and lime juice. Add the tomatoes then stir them into the avocado mixture along with the cilantro.

Assemble the bowls with the quinoa, a generous serving of the guacamole, the beans, and all the veggies. Squeeze over the lime juice and sprinkle with a few bits of cilantro. Add the chile and salt to your bowl, if you like.

DINNER TIME & FAMILY MEALS

If you don't want to feel like you are constantly making food for your baby, the easiest thing is for your family to all eat the same food from early on.

Getting the whole family to eat the same food has many benefits: you save time, you are exposing your baby to a wide range of flavors and textures, and you might also find that you all start eating a little healthier!

In this chapter I've set out some tried-and-tested meals that my family enjoys. I've also included some quick hacks—meals made from store-bought staples like wraps and pastry. Sometimes life needs a shortcut.

TIPS:
- When cooking dishes with veggies, cut some into larger batons to be used as finger food.
- When cooking one-pot dishes (like curries, soups, etc.) get into the habit of taking out your baby's portion before you add seasoning for older children and adults.
- Adapt the texture of dishes to suit the stage your baby is at. At the start of weaning you might blend or mash their portion. As your baby progresses, start to leave chunks and whole beans for them to pick up themselves.

DAL YOUR WAY

PREP: 5 mins
COOK: 45 mins
SERVES: 2 adults and
2 children (with some left to
freeze)

1 tsp coconut oil

½ tsp mustard seeds

¼ onion, peeled and finely
chopped

2 cloves garlic, peeled and
finely chopped

1 cup (190 g) split red
lentils, rinsed well

1-inch (3 cm) piece fresh
ginger, peeled and cut in
half

1 tsp ground turmeric

1 tsp ground cumin

We go through tons of lentils at home—they are high in protein and iron, versatile, and cheap. Dal is one of my favorite uses for lentils and it is the ultimate weaning food: simple, adaptable, and nourishing.

Once you have your base dal going, you can add lots of different vegetables to introduce your little one to different flavors and textures. Leafy greens and tomatoes are high in vitamin C so boost iron absorption. Adding greens right at the end of cooking will help to preserve the nutrients.

If you are baby-led weaning, you can thicken the dal for loaded spoons, either by cooking for slightly longer, using less water, or mixing through some cooked quinoa (which is an amazing extra protein boost). If your baby doesn't do well with loaded spoons, give them some veggies cut into chunky batons for them to hold and just let them dig in. You can also try serving the dal on strips of flatbread.

Heat the coconut oil in a large saucepan and add the mustard seeds. When the mustard seeds start to pop, add the onion and cook for about 10 minutes until softened. Add the garlic and cook for a couple of minutes.

Add the lentils and 3½ cups (820 ml) water, bring to a boil, and cook for about 3 minutes. Use a spoon to remove any scum that rises to the surface.

Add the ginger, turmeric, and cumin. If you are adding more vegetables (see box), add them now. Cover and simmer for around half an hour until the lentils are fully cooked.

Once the lentils are cooked add any optional greens (see box). Cook for about 5 minutes and then remove from the heat.

Remove the chunks of ginger before serving.

Serve with rice, quinoa, or flatbreads, topped with any of the optional serving toppings,* if you like.

Freeze any leftovers in individual baby-sized portions for instant ready meals.

OPTIONAL EXTRAS

- 1 cup of chopped vegetables e.g., pumpkin, carrot, butternut squash, and/or sweet potato. You could keep a few aside, cut into batons for baby-led weaning if you prefer. Otherwise, chop fairly small.
- Coconut milk. Switch 1½ cups (350 ml) of the cooking water for a can of coconut milk.
- Two handfuls of greens such as finely chopped kale, spinach, green beans, and/or peas.
- Add heat to your portion with some red pepper flakes and salt, if you like.
- * TOPPINGS: Add a squeeze of lemon, a few toasted nuts and seeds (make sure larger nuts and seeds are milled for babies), desiccated coconut, cilantro, yogurt.

PEA ORZOTTO

This is a mid-week staple of mine and one that the kids always polish off.
Frozen peas might seem like an innocuous filler vegetable but they are actually
a great source of protein and fiber. They are also great for a baby mastering
their pincer grasp (which generally occurs between 8 and 12 months).

If your baby isn't great with texture, you can blend their portion and top with
milled rather than whole pine nuts. If you are baby-led weaning you might
want to let the orzotto cool slightly and then roll your baby's portion into balls.

PREP: 5 minutes
COOK: 20 minutes
SERVES: 2 adults and 1 baby

4 tbsp pine nuts

1 tbsp olive oil

½ onion, peeled and finely chopped

½ zucchini, grated

1 clove garlic, peeled and chopped

½ cup (100 g) orzo

1½ cups (350 ml) low-salt stock

1 cup (140 g) frozen peas

Generous handful of grated cheese (leave out if dairy-free, or use 2 tbsp nutritional yeast)

Toast the pine nuts in a large frying pan over medium heat.
Keep stirring until they have a bit of color on all sides,
which will take about 2 minutes. Remove from the pan and
set aside.

Add the olive oil to the pan and heat. Add the onion and
cook for about 5 minutes. Add the zucchini and garlic and
cook for 1 minute more.

Add the orzo and stir for a minute, then add the stock.
Bring to a boil and then turn down to a low simmer. Cook
for about 10 minutes, stirring occasionally until the orzo is
cooked (it will be soft with no crunch left to it).

When the orzo is cooked, add the peas and cook for another
3 minutes until the peas are cooked. Turn the heat off, then
stir in the cheese, if using. Top with the toasted pine nuts
and serve.

SUBSTITUTIONS

I've used zucchini in this recipe but you can switch
this for ¼ head cauliflower or broccoli, finely chopped,
depending on what's available.

MAGIC CURRY

PREP: 15 minutes
COOK: 30 minutes
SERVES: 2 adults and
2 children

1 tbsp coconut oil

1 tsp mustard seeds

1 onion, peeled and finely
chopped

2 cloves garlic, peeled and
chopped

1-inch (3 cm) piece fresh
ginger, grated

¼ head cauliflower,
chopped into florets

½ sweet potato, peeled and
cut into ½-inch (1 cm)
cubes

1 tsp ground cumin

1 tsp ground coriander

1 tsp ground turmeric

1 tsp curry powder

One 15.5-ounce (400 g)
can chickpeas, drained
and rinsed

One 13.5-ounce (400 g)
can coconut milk

One 14.5-ounce (400 g)
can chopped tomatoes

Lime, yogurt, chiles, and
salt, to serve (optional)

Magic curry got its name because it was the first curry my son ever ate. It's a perfect introduction to curry—a slightly sweet sauce with warm spices running through. This is a very easy pantry curry and it freezes well so it's ideal to make up a batch on a rainy afternoon to add to your freezer stash.

Heat the coconut oil in a large saucepan over low heat until melted and then add the mustard seeds. When you hear the mustard seeds start to pop, add the onion. Cook the onion for about 10 minutes until soft. Add the garlic and ginger and cook for 2 minutes.

Add the cauliflower and sweet potato, along with the ground cumin, coriander, turmeric, and curry powder, and cook for 3 minutes. Then add the chickpeas, coconut milk, and tomatoes. Simmer the curry for about 25 minutes until the vegetables are cooked.

For young and spoon-fed babies, gently mash or blend their portion. Once your baby's pincer grasp is developed you can leave the curry with more texture for them to pick up chickpeas, vegetables, etc.

Serve with quinoa, rice, or a flatbread, a squeeze of lime, and a spoonful of yogurt. Add salt and fresh chile to adult portions.

SUBSTITUTIONS

I've written the recipe using cauliflower and sweet potato but you can replace these with any other vegetables you like. You can also add some greens toward the end of cooking; spinach and/or peas are both delicious, and they only take 5 minutes to cook.

SWEET POTATO TOSTADAS WITH BLACK BEAN DIP

PREP: 15 minutes
COOK: 25 minutes
SERVES: 2 adults and 1 baby.
Makes 8–10 tostadas

1 large sweet potato, cut into ½-inch (1 cm) rounds (no need to peel)

½ tsp olive oil

1 clove garlic, peeled and chopped

½ tsp ground coriander

½ tsp ground cumin

One 15.5-ounce (400 g) can black beans, with half the liquid drained

½ tsp low-salt bouillon powder

TOPPINGS
(choose as many as you like)

3 tomatoes, chopped

1 avocado, peeled and diced

Chopped roasted peppers

Small handful of shredded lettuce or cabbage

Cilantro

Lime

Corn kernels

Handful of grated cheese

Sour cream

ADULTS
Salt, chiles (chipotle sauce is excellent!)

A lot of my recipes come from food that I loved pre-baby and that I wanted my baby to enjoy, too. I got hooked on black bean dip (or frijoles) years ago when I was backpacking through Mexico and Central America. I might have forgotten all the Spanish I learned then, but I remember the black beans.

Tostadas are like crispy tacos. In this version I've used sweet potato rounds, which are a much easier texture for babies to eat and they mash well if you want to spoon-feed them.

Preheat the oven to 400°F (200°C).

Place the sweet potato slices on a large baking sheet and bake for 25 minutes (you don't need any oil).

Meanwhile, heat the olive oil in a saucepan over low heat. Add the garlic and gently fry for a few minutes. Add the ground coriander and cumin and cook for another minute.

Add the beans (with half the liquid from the can) and bouillon powder. Gently simmer for around 10 minutes, then mash.

When the sweet potato is cooked, assemble your tostadas. Spread around 1 tablespoon of the black beans on each, then add any toppings you'd like.

If your baby is very young, cut the tostadas into strips for baby-led weaning or gently mash for spoon-feeding.

SUBSTITUTIONS

If you prefer you can use regular white potatoes. Choose large ones so that the rounds are a decent size.

CASHEW NOODLES

8+

PREP: 5 minutes
COOK: 10 minutes
SERVES: 2 adults and 1 baby

Two 2-ounce (50g) nests whole wheat noodles

1 tsp toasted sesame oil

¼ onion, peeled and finely chopped

½ zucchini, grated

1 carrot, peeled and grated

Handful of finely shredded cabbage

1-inch (3 cm) piece fresh ginger, peeled and grated

2 cloves garlic, peeled and chopped

Handful of cashews, crushed (toasted if you have time)

Soy sauce and/or red pepper flakes, for adults, if you like

CASHEW SAUCE

2 tbsp cashew butter

1 tsp toasted sesame oil

2 tbsp coconut milk or water

Juice of ½ lime

If you've got a hangry baby situation, this dish is perfect. This is a very simple and quick dish, but thanks to the cashew sauce it's still providing some all-important protein.

For babies who haven't mastered their pincer grasp, serve some steamed batons of carrot and zucchini alongside the noodles, which will be easier for them to pick up.

Bring a pan of water to a boil and cook your noodles following the instructions on the package. When they are cooked, drain and set them aside.

Meanwhile, mix together the ingredients for your cashew sauce and set aside.

Heat the sesame oil in a large saucepan (or wok) over medium to high heat. Add the onion, zucchini, carrot, and cabbage and cook for about 3 minutes, stirring constantly. Add the ginger and garlic and cook for another 2 minutes.

Add the cooked noodles and mix well. Cook for 2 minutes, then pour the cashew sauce over. Cook for another minute and transfer to bowls.

Sprinkle with the crushed cashews. Add soy sauce and/or red pepper flakes for adults, if you like.

SUBSTITUTIONS

The following veggies all work well in this stir-fry if you want to mix it up a bit:

- Broccoli
- Cauliflower
- Bok choy/pak choi
- Pepper
- Peas and corn
- Green beans and snow peas

If your baby has a tree nut allergy, make up the sauce without the cashew butter and instead add some egg or tofu for more protein.

SUMMER ROLLS

8+

PREP: 30 minutes +
10 minutes rolling
(plus 2 hours resting)
COOK: 20 minutes
MAKES: 9 rolls (4 per adult
and 1 for baby)

1 block (10 ounces/280 g)
  firm tofu (preferably
  organic), cut into ½-inch
  (1 cm) batons
1 tbsp cornstarch
One 2-ounce (45 g) nest
  brown rice vermicelli
  noodles
1 avocado, mashed
1 carrot, peeled and grated
¼ cucumber, grated
2 tbsp sesame seeds
1 package rice paper sheets
  (you won't use all of them
  but there might be some
  broken ones in the pack)

MARINADE FOR TOFU
Juice of 1 lime
1 tbsp toasted sesame oil
1-inch (3 cm) piece ginger,
  peeled and grated
1 clove garlic, peeled and
  chopped

OPTIONAL
Satay dipping sauce (see
  page 113)
For adults: Soy sauce/
  tamari, for dipping

Summer rolls are a very delicious, fresh dinner, and a wonderful sensory experience (read: messy). Full disclosure: rice paper sheets can be a bit of a pain to wrap if you haven't done it before; I'd caution against making this dish for the first time if you are feeling in any way fraught or over-tired (speaking from experience . . .). If it's your first time rolling a summer roll, take a quick look at an online demo so you can see how to roll.

Tofu is a great plant-based source of protein, iron, and calcium, but it has a bit of a bad rep for being quite bland. This simple (salt-free) marinade will give it a bit of zing, plus the ginger provides great immune support. If you don't have the time or energy, these are tasty without the marinating, too.

I grated the veggies in this recipe, which makes them easier for babies without teeth. However, if your baby is older you can slice the vegetables into thin batons.

Mix together the marinade ingredients, if using. Put the tofu into a bowl and pour the marinade over it. Gently mix until the tofu is coated and place in the fridge for about 2 hours.

Preheat the oven to 400°F (200°C). Add the cornstarch to the tofu and mix gently. Place the tofu on a baking pan and bake for around 15–20 minutes until it's starting to crisp.

Meanwhile, cook the noodles according to the instructions on the package. Once they are cooked drain them immediately and set aside.

Recipe continues →

SUMMER ROLLS
CONTINUED

Put some warm water in a shallow dish. Put a clean board next to the bowl to do your wrapping.

Have your fillings lined up ready to go in this order: avocado, tofu, carrot, cucumber, noodles, sesame seeds. Dip a rice paper sheet into the water for a few seconds until it is soft, then lay it on your board.

In the center of the paper, spoon mashed avocado in a rectangle (about 3 × 1 inches/8 × 3 cm). Put 2 strips of tofu on top followed by a little cucumber, carrot, noodles, and sesame seeds. Don't overfill the rice paper otherwise it will be hard to roll.

Fold over the two end sides, then fold over the side closest to you to cover the ingredients (slightly tucking it under the fillings) and then roll up (rolling away from you).

Serve with a satay sauce (see page 113) or some soy sauce for the adults.

QUICK HACKS WITH PUFF PASTRY

Puff pastry is a great texture for little ones; it can be messy to eat, but it's nice for babies to grab and the texture means it melts in their mouths. The salt content of store-bought pastry means I wouldn't use it every day, but once in a while it makes a great quick dinner. Here are a few things I like to make with puff pastry.

TARTS

PREP: 10 minutes
COOK: 15 minutes
MAKES: 6 tarts

WHAT YOU NEED
1½ sheets from a 17.3-ounce (490 g) package frozen puff pastry, defrosted
Veggie-loaded tomato sauce (see page 105) or pesto (see page 94)
3 handfuls of veggies (e.g., roasted sliced peppers, zucchini, mushrooms, asparagus, tomatoes)
2 tbsp grated cheese/ nutritional yeast
Olive oil, for brushing

Mix and match to make these tarts, depending on what you have on hand. I like to use roasted veggies such as eggplant, peppers, and zucchini, and sometimes a raw veggie, such as asparagus, when in season.

LET'S COOK
Preheat the oven to 400°F (200°C) and line a baking sheet with parchment paper.

Cut the pastry into squares, about 4 × 4 inches (10 × 10 cm). Put the squares on the baking sheet and score a line ½ inch (1 cm) in from each edge of the tart (this allows the outside to puff up). Spread the tomato sauce or pesto inside the scored square, and sprinkle the vegetables on top. Sprinkle on the cheese or yeast. Brush the edges with olive oil.

Bake for around 15 minutes until the edges are puffed up and golden.

PASTRY PARCELS

PREP: 10 minutes
COOK: 20 minutes
MAKES: 6 parcels

You can use all the same veggies as in the tarts, but you fold these to make handy little parcels. Perfect for finger food and for packed lunches.

WHAT YOU NEED

1½ sheets from a 17.3-ounce (490 g) package frozen puff pastry, defrosted
Leftover baked beans (see page 142), veggie chili (see page 146) or any vegetable of your choice!
Handful of grated cheese
Olive oil, for brushing

LET'S COOK

Preheat the oven to 400°F (200°C) and line a baking sheet with parchment paper.

Cut the pastry into squares about 4 × 4 inches (10 × 10 cm). Imagine a line running diagonally from corner to corner. Add 2 tablespoons of filling and a small handful of grated cheese to one side. Then fold it in half diagonally. Use a fork to press the pastry together. Pierce a couple of holes in the top using a fork and brush with olive oil.

Place the parcels on the baking sheet and bake for about 15–20 minutes until the pastry is puffed and golden.

PINWHEELS

PREP: 10 minutes
COOK: 15 minutes
MAKES: 12 pinwheels

These are more of a snack than a dinner, but I wanted to include them as a useful puff pastry hack. Again, these are an excellent way to use up leftover sauces.

WHAT YOU NEED

1½ sheets from a 17.3-ounce (490 g) package frozen puff pastry, defrosted
4 tbsp leftover sauce or pesto (see page 94)
Handful of cheese or nutritional yeast
2 tbsp mini seeds (e.g., hulled hemp or sesame)
Olive oil, for brushing

LET'S COOK

Preheat the oven to 400°F (200°C) and line a baking sheet with parchment paper.

Spread the sauce over the top of the pastry sheet. Sprinkle on the cheese or yeast and seeds. Roll up the pastry starting from the long edge closest to you. Using a sharp knife, cut the pastry into slices around 1 inch (3 cm) thick (be fairly gentle so it doesn't squash down too much). Arrange on the baking sheet with the flat sides down. Brush with olive oil and bake for around 15 minutes until the pastry is puffed and golden.

TARTS, PASTRY PARCELS & PINWHEELS (pages 136–137)

LENTIL BALLS WITH TOMATO SAUCE

PREP: 15 minutes
COOK: 50 minutes
SERVES: 2 adults and
2 children. Makes 18 balls

Ideal first food (finger food)

1 tsp olive oil

½ onion, peeled and finely chopped

1 clove garlic, peeled and crushed

One 15-ounce (425 g) can brown lentils, drained and rinsed

½ cup (40 g) oats

3 white button mushrooms, roughly chopped

1 carrot, peeled and grated

Zest of ½ lemon

1 tsp dried oregano (or a couple of sprigs of fresh)

TOMATO SAUCE

1 tsp olive oil

½ onion, peeled and finely chopped

2 cloves garlic, peeled and chopped

Two 14.5-ounce (410 g) cans chopped tomatoes

½ tsp balsamic vinegar

1 tsp dried oregano (or a couple of sprigs of fresh)

Fresh parsley, to serve

Crisp on the outside and soft in the middle, these lentil balls are perfect for little hands to grab. Unassuming-looking, they are packed with good stuff: lentils, oats, mushrooms, and carrots. The combination of plant-based protein and fiber gives a slow, steady energy release for a hearty, filling meal. With the tomato sauce they are great by themselves, or you can serve with spaghetti or some fresh bread.

I make these in a food processor, but an immersion blender will work, too—just chop the veggies up a little smaller.

Preheat the oven to 400°F (200°C) and line a large baking sheet with parchment paper.

Heat the olive oil in a pan and gently fry the onions for about 10 minutes until softened. Add the garlic and cook for 2 minutes before turning off the heat.

While the onion is cooking, put all the other lentil ball ingredients in a food processor (or in a bowl if using an immersion blender). Add the cooked onions and blend. You want the mix to have a bit of texture so don't blend it until completely smooth.

Shape the mixture into 18 small golf ball–sized balls and put them on your baking sheet. Bake the balls for about 35 minutes until they are crisp on the outside (but still soft in the middle).

While the balls are cooking make the tomato sauce. Heat the olive oil over medium heat in a pan and add the onion. Cook the onion for about 10 minutes until softened. Add the garlic and cook for another 2 minutes. Then add the chopped tomato, ½ cup (120 ml) water, the balsamic vinegar, and oregano. Cook the mixture over low heat for about 10–15 minutes until thickened.

Serve the balls with the sauce poured over, and a little freshly chopped parsley.

If you want to freeze or store for a later meal, keep the balls and the sauce separate (the balls will become too soft otherwise).

BAKED BEANS & MINI POTATOES

PREP: 5 minutes
COOK: 35 minutes
SERVES: 2 adults and
2 children (with some left over to freeze)

Ideal first food (mashed/ blended)

Small baking potatoes, 2 per adult, 1 per baby
1 tsp olive oil
½ onion, peeled and finely chopped
1 carrot, peeled and finely chopped
1 stick celery, finely chopped
1 clove garlic, peeled and chopped
½ tsp paprika
One 14.5-ounce (410 g) can chopped tomatoes
1 tsp balsamic vinegar
One 14.5-ounce (410 g) can navy beans (water retained)
One 15.5-ounce (440 g) can navy beans, drained and rinsed
Grated cheese, avocado, or yogurt, to serve (optional)

First things first—these baked beans do not taste like the ordinary canned ones, and they aren't baked (they are cooked on the stove). But they are salt- and sugar-free, they've got added veggies, and they taste good—so perfect for babies! Served with mini potatoes, because is there anything better than a baked potato and beans?

Rich in protein and complex carbs (which keep your baby fuller for longer), plus iron, folate, and magnesium, beans are an excellent meal for your growing baby.

Preheat the oven to 400°F (200°C). Put the potatoes on a baking pan and bake in the oven for around 35 minutes (until soft).

Heat the oil in a large saucepan over medium heat. Add the onion and cook for 5 minutes until softened. Then add the carrot and celery and cook for 10 minutes more, taking care not to let the mixture burn. Add the garlic and paprika and cook for another 2 minutes.

Add the chopped tomatoes and balsamic vinegar. Bring to a boil then turn down the heat and gently simmer for 10 minutes. If you want your tomato sauce to be smooth, leave to cool a little and then blend before you add the beans. Return the sauce to the saucepan.

Add the beans and simmer the beans for around 10 minutes.

Serve the beans with your mini potatoes. Add cheese, avocado, or a splotch of natural yogurt, if you like.

If you are spoon-feeding, scoop out a tablespoon of the soft potato and mix with some mashed beans.

Freeze leftover beans in baby-size portions for instant meals!

QUINOA VEGGIE FRIES & HOMEMADE KETCHUP

PREP: 20 minutes
COOK: 30 minutes
MAKES: 24 fries

Ideal first food (finger food)

½ eggplant
½ zucchini
½ sweet potato
¾ cup (45 g) bread crumbs
¾ cup (75 g) quinoa flakes
½ tsp paprika
4 tbsp (25 g) flour (any kind)
2 eggs, beaten (or 2 flax egg wash, see page 182)
Olive oil, for drizzling

HOMEMADE KETCHUP
1 tsp olive oil
1 small carrot, peeled and grated
½ apple, peeled and grated
1 clove garlic, peeled and chopped
One 14.5-ounce (410 g) can chopped tomatoes
½ tsp paprika
½ tsp balsamic vinegar

These veggie fries are a great way of introducing your baby to lots of different vegetables. They are a perfect first food as the crumbed outside makes them easy to grip, as well as giving your baby some additional fiber and protein.

The homemade ketchup is my favorite accompaniment. Sugar- and salt-free and veggie-loaded, it's an amazing baby-friendly alternative to store-bought ketchups.

Preheat the oven to 400°F (200°C) and line a large baking sheet with parchment paper.

Cut the eggplant, zucchini, and sweet potato into french fry shapes (each makes around 8 wedges).

Mix together the bread crumbs, quinoa flakes, and paprika.

Set up three bowls. Put the flour in one, the beaten eggs in the second, and the bread crumb mixture in the last. Dip each fry first in the flour, then the egg, and finally the crumb mixture, and place on the baking sheet. You want each one to be fully coated.

Drizzle a little olive oil over them. Bake for about 30 minutes until they are golden and crispy.

Meanwhile, make the ketchup. Heat the olive oil in a saucepan over medium heat. Add the grated carrot and apple. Cook for a few minutes and then add the garlic and cook for 1 minute more. Add the remaining ingredients to the pan. Bring the mixture to a boil and then turn down and gently simmer for 15 minutes. Remove from the heat and leave to cool a little before blending until smooth.

ONE-POT VEGGIE QUINOA CHILI

PREP: 10 minutes
COOK: 1 hour 10 minutes
SERVES: 2 adults and
2 children (with some left
to freeze)

Ideal first food (mashed/
blended)

½ tbsp olive oil

½ onion, peeled and
finely chopped

2 cloves garlic, peeled
and chopped

3 white button
mushrooms, chopped

½ red pepper, finely
chopped

½ sweet potato, peeled
and finely chopped

1 tsp ground cumin

½ tsp ground coriander

½ tsp sweet smoked
paprika

¼ tsp ground allspice

One 15.5-ounce
(440 g) can black
beans (including the
liquid)

One 14.5-ounce
(410 g) can chopped
tomatoes

⅓ cup (60 g) quinoa

I love chili as it's basically a big pot of goodness. This version is great for babies—it's full of different veggies, beans, and quinoa—which are a veggie lifeline for protein and iron (a squeeze of lime juice before serving will help maximize iron absorption).

I've listed some toppings you can try; they provide a bit of extra nutrition, and as your baby gets older, especially when they go through fussy phases, giving them control over what toppings they add gives them some autonomy.

Heat the oil in a large saucepan and add the onion. Cook for around 10 minutes until softened, then add the garlic and cook for a couple of minutes. Add the mushrooms, red pepper, and sweet potato and the cumin, coriander, paprika, and allspice. Cook for about 3 minutes.

Add the beans, tomatoes, quinoa, and 1 cup (240 ml) water. Turn up the heat and bring the mixture to a boil. Then turn the heat down to low, put a lid on the pan and cook for around 45 minutes (stirring occasionally) until the sweet potato is cooked through. Serve with as many toppings as you like.

OPTIONAL TOPPINGS

- Full-fat natural yogurt, sour cream, or dairy-free yogurt
- Corn
- Grated cheese
- Nutritional yeast
- Slices of avocado

- Cilantro
- Lime
- Chiles and salt (for adults)

Feel free to adapt the veggies to what you have in the fridge. You can also use whatever beans you like.

VEDGEREE

PREP: 25 minutes
COOK: 40 minutes
SERVES: 2 adults and
2 children

½ cup (80 g) brown rice

½ cup (80 g) dried red split
  lentils

1 tsp coconut oil

½ onion, finely chopped

2 cloves garlic, peeled and
  chopped

2 tsp curry powder

1-inch (3 cm) piece ginger,
  peeled and finely grated

2 carrots, peeled and diced
  or cut into batons

4 eggs, to serve (optional)

¼ head broccoli, chopped
  into small florets

¼ head cauliflower,
  chopped into small
  florets

¼ cup (35 g) peas, frozen
  or canned

¼ cup (35 g) corn, frozen
  or canned

Fresh parsley, chopped, to
  serve (optional)

Salt, black pepper, and red
  pepper flakes, to serve
  (optional)

This is a hybrid between a standard kedgeree, which usually contains smoked fish, and the dish from which kedgeree originated, kitchari, which is made with rice and lentils. It's great for babies as it's packed with veggies and protein and has a lovely light spice (I'm a big believer in introducing babies to spices and curries!).

Using brown rice will make the dish higher in fiber, but if you are short of time you can use basmati rice and reduce the cooking time by half.

Rinse the rice and lentils in a colander under running water.

Heat the coconut oil in a large frying pan over medium heat. When the coconut oil is hot add the onion and garlic and cook for a couple of minutes. Then add the curry powder and ginger and cook for another 2 minutes.

Add the carrots and stir so that they are coated in the spice mix. Add the rice and lentils to the pan. Stir, add 2 cups (470 ml) fresh water, and bring to a boil. Once the mixture is boiling, turn down to a low simmer, cover, and cook for about 25 minutes, stirring occasionally. If the mixture is looking too dry, then add some more water.

If you are adding eggs cook these now. Boil the eggs for 10 minutes and then run under cold water before peeling. Cut into quarters.

When the rice has been cooking for 25 minutes, add the broccoli and cauliflower. Mix and cook for 5 minutes until the broccoli is soft. Then add the peas and corn and cook for another couple of minutes and remove from the heat.

Serve with some chopped parsley and/or boiled egg, if using.

Grown-ups: add salt, pepper, and chile flakes to serve.

QUICK HACKS WITH WRAPS

Store-bought wraps make great quick dinner hacks—
they are versatile and very quick to cook. There are
lots of gluten-free options on the market if your baby
is allergic to wheat.

QUESADILLA

PREP: 5 minutes
COOK: 10 minutes
MAKES: 1

WHAT YOU NEED
1 wrap

SUGGESTED FILLINGS
Handful of grated cheese
½ sweet potato, steamed
   and mashed
2 tbsp cooked kidney beans
   or lentils, mashed
2 tbsp black bean dip (see
   page 131)
½ avocado, mashed
Handful of cooked peas or
   corn

These are made by folding a filled wrap and cooking in
a pan on the stove. You can use a variety of different
fillings. Although a quesadilla traditionally contains
cheese, it doesn't have to. Mashed sweet potato/
pumpkin is a great substitute for cheese in these.

LET'S COOK
Heat up a large frying pan (big enough to fit your wrap in)
over medium heat on the stove. When the pan is hot put
the wrap in the pan.

Scatter your chosen toppings over one half (don't overfill
otherwise the fillings will seep out as it cooks). Fold the
other side of the wrap over and press down. Cook for
a couple of minutes until the bottom becomes slightly
golden. Flip the quesadilla over carefully and cook the other
side for a couple of minutes until it turns golden. If you are
using cheese you want the cheese to melt inside and the
quesadilla to stick together.

Cut into small strips for your baby to grab.

TACO BOWL

PREP: 5 minutes
COOK: 10 minutes
MAKES: 1

WHAT YOU NEED
1 small round wrap, about
    6 inches (15 cm) in
    diameter

SUGGESTED FILLINGS
Cooked quinoa or rice, chili,
baked beans, or any of the
suggested fillings for the
quesadilla (see page 148)

When you are weaning a baby there will be numerous
times you'll think: "If only the bowl was food!"—and this
time it is!

It's best if you can buy mini wraps as the bowl will be
a better size for a baby, but if you can't you can cut a
larger one down to size.

LET'S COOK
Preheat the oven to 350°F (180°C). Push the wrap into a
muffin pan cup and then bake for around 10 minutes (until
the wrap holds its shape). Remove from the pan and fill
with your choice of fillings.

PIZZA

PREP: 5 minutes
COOK: 10 minutes
MAKES: 1

WHAT YOU NEED
1 wrap
2 tbsp veggie-loaded
    tomato sauce (see page
    105), pesto (page 94), or
    tomato purée
Handful of grated cheese
Handful of grated zucchini
Any other veggie toppings
    you enjoy

Using a wrap for a base makes a super-quick pizza. This is
especially good for using up any little bits of pasta sauce
or pesto, or just take a few cubes out of your freezer
stash. Tomato purée also works fine if you don't have
anything else to use up.

LET'S COOK
Preheat the oven to 400°F (200°C) and line a baking pan
with parchment paper.

Put the wrap on the baking pan. Spread your base sauce
over to reach the edges. Top with the cheese and zucchini,
and add any other veggies, if using. Bake in the oven for
around 8–10 minutes until the cheese has melted and the
base is crispy.

SUBSTITUTIONS: If you don't want to add cheese, cooked
and mashed sweet potato and a sprinkling of nutritional
yeast is nice on these pizzas, too.

TACO BOWLS (page 149)

MUSHROOM (MISO) BROTH

PREP: 10 minutes
COOK: 25 minutes
SERVES: 2 adults and 1 baby

Ideal first food (blended)

Handful of dried
   mushrooms (e.g., porcini)
3 eggs (or baked tofu, see
   page 133)
1 tsp toasted sesame oil
2 cloves garlic, peeled and
   chopped
2-inch (5 cm) piece fresh
   ginger, peeled and grated
Handful of white button
   mushrooms, sliced
2 cups (500 ml) low-salt
   stock
Half an ear corn on the cob,
   cut into slices about 1 inch
   (3 cm) thick
3 ounces (100 g) noodles
   (soba is a good choice)
1 tsp crispy seaweed flakes
   (optional)
Sesame seeds, to decorate

OPTIONAL EXTRAS FOR ADULTS/OLDER CHILDREN

1 tbsp miso paste
1 scallion, finely chopped
Red pepper flakes or fresh
   chile, chopped

Little ones, especially those with older siblings, can pick up bugs and inevitably they pass their bugs on to you! Broth is your answer! Ready incredibly quickly, broth is very soothing and nourishing. Plus your baby will enjoy fishing out the various ingredients.

Mushrooms are an ideal base for broth as they are rich in flavor, as well as delivering some B vitamins and the antioxidant selenium, which supports the immune system. If you can get hold of it, a little seaweed sprinkled over at the end provides a bit of texture and a new taste; it's also rich in nutrients including calcium and iodine. You can use baked tofu (see page 133) instead of eggs, if you like.

Put the dried mushrooms in a bowl, pour ½ cup (120 ml) boiling water over them, and leave to soak.

Bring a pan of water (enough to cover the eggs) to a boil and then gently lower your eggs into it. Boil for 7 minutes and then empty the water and pour cold water over them. Leave them to cool in the cold water.

Meanwhile, heat the toasted sesame oil in a saucepan over medium heat. Add the garlic and ginger, and cook for 2 minutes. Then add the fresh mushrooms and cook for about 3 minutes. Add the stock. Bring to a boil and then turn down to a gentle simmer and cook for about 5 minutes.

Remove your dried mushrooms from the hot water (keep the water). Chop finely, and add to the broth. Add the mushroom water to the broth (leave a little bit in the bottom of the bowl as this will contain the grit from the mushrooms).

Recipe continues →

MUSHROOM (MISO) BROTH CONTINUED

Add the corn and cook for 2 minutes, and then add the noodles. Cook until the noodles are soft (the package will give cooking times).

Peel the boiled eggs and cut into halves.

Spoon your baby's broth into a bowl (if your baby isn't great with texture, then blend their portion before adding the toppings). Add half an egg, a pinch of seaweed, and some sesame seeds, if using.

For the adult portions, remove a little of the broth with a mug and stir in the miso paste until combined. Return the miso mix to the pan and stir in. Ladle into bowls. Top with egg, seaweed, sesame seeds, chopped scallion, and chile, if using.

SUBSTITUTIONS

You can add lots of different veggies to vary this broth. Broccoli, green beans, sugar snap peas, and carrots are all great. Just add a handful when you add the noodles.

EASY BUTTERNUT RISOTTO

PREP: 10 minutes
COOK: 1 hour (30 minutes for white rice)
SERVES: 2 adults and 2 children (with some left over to freeze)

½ medium butternut squash

1 tbsp olive oil, plus a little more to rub squash with

½ onion, peeled and finely chopped

2 cloves garlic, peeled and chopped

1 cup (190 g) brown rice, rinsed well

3½ cups (850 ml) low-salt stock

2 tbsp nutritional yeast or small handful of grated cheese (optional)

I love risotto; it's comfort food at its best, and my kids love it, too. The roasted butternut in this one makes it deliciously creamy, without the need to stir it continually.

If you use brown rice it does take longer to cook, but once it is simmering it is not too labor-intensive. If you want to use white rice or risotto rice the cooking time will be more like 25 minutes.

Preheat the oven to 350°F (180°C).

Cut diagonal lines into your butternut squash. Rub with olive oil and place on a baking sheet. Bake for around 45 minutes until soft (check on it occasionally to ensure it doesn't burn). Once it is cooked remove from the oven and set aside to cool.

Meanwhile, heat the olive oil in a large frying pan or medium saucepan and add the onion. Cook for around 10 minutes until softened, then add the garlic and cook for about 2 minutes.

Add the brown rice to the pan and stir well. Add 3 cups (700 ml) of the stock, bring it to a boil and then turn the pan down to a low simmer and cover. Cook for 35–45 minutes, checking every 7–8 minutes or so and giving it a stir. Add the remaining stock if it's starting to look a little dry. When the rice is cooked, most of the stock will have been absorbed and the rice will no longer be crunchy to taste.

Scoop the flesh of the butternut out of the skin and stir into the rice.

Turn off the heat and then stir in the nutritional yeast or cheese.

SWEET POTATO "QUICHE"

This is cross between a quiche and a Spanish omelette. The filling is your typical quiche filling, but the crust is thin slices of sweet potato instead of pastry, which means no pastry making, no rolling, no blind-baking! It also delivers a nice boost of gut-friendly fiber and immune-supporting beta-carotene.

Using sweet potato slices as opposed to pastry means that the quiche filling seeps through a bit so bear that in mind when choosing a dish to cook it in (i.e. don't choose anything with a loose bottom or holes!).

PREP: 15 minutes
COOK: 45 minutes
SERVES: 2 adults and
2 children

Ideal first food (finger food)

1 large sweet potato, cut into slices about ¼ inch (5 mm) thick

1 tsp olive oil, plus extra for greasing

1 leek, finely chopped

2 large handfuls of fresh spinach, finely chopped (or 4 tbsp frozen, defrosted)

Handful of grated cheese

4 eggs

1 cup (240 ml) milk of your choice

Preheat the oven to 400°F (200°C).

Grease a 9-inch (23 cm) quiche or ovenproof dish with oil, and then line with the sweet potato slices; overlap the slices to make a circle, starting from the center of the dish. You can cut the slices in half to make them fit if you need to.

Heat the olive oil in a frying pan, then add the leek and cook for about 10 minutes until softened. Then add the spinach and cook for about 3 minutes until it's wilted.

Spread the leek and spinach mix over the potato layer and then sprinkle a handful of grated cheese over.

Whisk together the eggs and milk and pour over the cheese. Brush any sweet potatoes that are sticking out with more olive oil. Then bake for 25–30 minutes until the filling is cooked through; it will be golden and with no wobble.

Leave to cool slightly before serving. Cut into baton-size slices for finger food for younger babies.

SUBSTITUTIONS

Mushrooms, asparagus, and broccoli are all excellent substitutions in this, either alongside the spinach, or on their own.

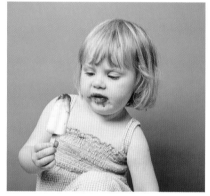

SWEET STUFF

First things first: Nothing in this chapter contains added sugar. Your baby doesn't need actual sugar. This chapter does contain some ways you can work with fruit (and veggies!) to create some delicious, nutrient-dense, and appealing desserts. Everything in this chapter could also be listed under snacks or breakfast.

When your baby is teething, food like ice pops and nice creams can soothe gums and provide a lot of comfort, so don't be afraid to offer them more often than you would usually.

I won't lie, I have a terrible sweet tooth. So for me, weaning was a great way to cast a light on some of my own food choices. I try not to eat anything in front of my children that I wouldn't be prepared to share with them, so this chapter is perhaps more about satisfying my own sweet tooth in a way that I am happy to share with my children.

APPLE SAUCE

PREP: 5 minutes
COOK: 20 minutes
MAKES: about 1 cup
(240 ml) apple sauce

3 eating apples, peeled,
    cored, and diced
1 tsp cinnamon

Apple sauce is great stirred through yogurt or on top of oatmeal (see page 39) or rice pudding (see page 164). It is also excellent to use in sweet baked goods and has the added benefit of acting like a binder, so it can be an egg substitute if you are egg-free or vegan.

Once you've made up a batch, it's a good idea to freeze it in an ice cube tray in individual portions (an ice cube works out to be roughly 1 tablespoon of sauce).

Pears work well, too, and this recipe is a great way of using up any elderly apples and pears in the fruit bowl.

Add all the ingredients with ½ cup (120 ml) water to a saucepan over medium heat. Bring to a boil and then turn down to a gentle simmer. Cook for about 30 minutes until the apples are soft and starting to fall apart. Stir occasionally to ensure the mixture doesn't stick.

Leave to cool and then blend, if needed.

ICE POPS

PREP: 5 minutes (plus
2 hours or overnight freezing)
Each mix makes around 4–6
ice pops depending on the
size of molds

My children eat ice pops all year round. Ice pops are the ultimate in sustainable eating—reusable molds, no plastic wrappers, and a great way to use up fruit that is leftover or past its best. They are also a wonderful sensory experience—bright colors, cold to the touch, and all those drips—perfection!

Keep an eye out for wrinkly fruit that has been marked down in the stores—these are perfect for ice pops (and jam, see page 166).

MANGO & COCONUT

1 super-ripe mango, peeled, pitted, roughly chopped
Half a 13.5-ounce can (200 ml) coconut milk

LET'S COOK

Put the mango and coconut milk in a blender and blend until smooth. Pour into molds and freeze.

BEET POP

2 handfuls of strawberries or raspberries
1 small cooked beet
A few drops of vanilla extract or ½ tsp vanilla bean paste (optional)
1 cup (240 ml) natural yogurt of your choice

LET'S COOK

Put the strawberries and beet and 2 tablespoons water in a blender and blend until smooth. Pour into your molds until about halfway up. If you are using vanilla, mix it with the yogurt. Top the molds with yogurt and freeze.

THE HULK

1 banana, peeled and chopped
1 pear or apple, peeled, cored, and chopped
1 tbsp frozen or a handful of fresh spinach
1 cup (240 ml) coconut water (just use water if you don't have coconut water)

LET'S COOK

Put everything in a blender and blend until smooth. Pour into molds and freeze.

ICE POPS (page 161)

COCONUT & CARDAMOM STOVE-TOP RICE PUDDING

Rice pudding, for me, is the ultimate comfort food. This version is made with coconut milk so it is dairy-free but just as creamy and delicious as regular rice pudding. I've also made it with a mix of brown rice and quinoa to up the protein and fiber content.

It tastes great on its own, but to make it even more decadent you could add some quick berry compote (see page 167), apple sauce (see page 160), or mango chia jam (see page 166).

PREP: 3 minutes
COOK: 30 minutes (20 minutes if you use white rice)
SERVES: 2 adults and 1 baby

One 13.5-ounce (400 ml) can coconut milk
6 tbsp brown rice, rinsed well
3 tbsp whole quinoa
½ tsp ground cardamom

Put all the ingredients into a small saucepan over medium heat and bring to a boil. Turn down to a simmer and cook for about 30 minutes until the coconut milk is mostly absorbed and the rice is cooked through.

Spoon into bowls and serve warm (wearing PJs for maximum comfort!).

Add some toppings if you like or a drizzle of maple syrup for the adults.

SUBSTITUTIONS

If you don't like coconut milk you can make this with any regular milk of your choice. It won't be as naturally sweet so you will almost certainly want to add a topping.

MANGO CHIA JAM

PREP: 10 minutes
MAKES: ½ cup

1 super-ripe mango, peeled,
   pitted, and roughly
   chopped
1 tbsp chia seeds

Chia is a pretty magical seed. It is high in protein and fiber and contains that all-important omega-3 fatty acid, which is a great brain food.

Mango chia jam is my absolute favorite chia jam. Mostly because it requires *no cooking* at all; you just blend the mango and done. This is best made with super-ripe, wrinkly mangos for juiciness and to help avoid food waste!

Put the mango into a blender and blend until smooth. Stir through the chia seeds. Leave for 5 minutes to thicken and then stir again before serving.

Will keep for around 5 days in an airtight container in the fridge, or freeze into individual portions using an ice cube tray.

Serve on toast, oats, yogurt, or straight up!

SUBSTITUTIONS

You can make chia jam with most fruits. Berries work really well as they are already naturally sweet so you won't need to add any additional sweetener for your baby. To make either blueberry, strawberry, or raspberry chia jam you will need to cook a cup of berries in a few tablespoons of water for about 5 minutes. Leave to cool a little, blend until smooth and then stir through 1 tablespoon of chia seeds.

QUICK BERRY COMPOTE

PREP: 5 minutes
COOK: 10 minutes
MAKES: ½ cup

1 apple or pear, peeled, cored, and diced
Generous handful of frozen blueberries
2 tbsp water
½ tsp cinnamon

A quick compote is perfect for dolloping onto plain yogurt for dessert, on oats for breakfast, or just on its own. I've used blueberries but you could use any berries you have.

This freezes well and I'd recommended spooning it into an ice cube tray so you have individual portions on hand instantly (especially great for cooling down hot oatmeal in the morning).

Put all the ingredients into a small saucepan and bring to a boil. Turn the heat down and gently simmer for about 10 minutes until the apple is soft and the berries are mushy. Leave to cool a little before serving. If you want it completely smooth you can blend it.

NICE CREAM

Frozen fruit is key here. You can either buy bags of frozen fruit or chop up some fresh fruit into fairly small chunks and freeze it overnight. Pineapple is especially good to freeze as you rarely get through a whole one at once.

PREP: 5 minutes

MAKES: ½ to 1 cup (120 to 240 ml)

TOPPINGS: sesame seeds, crushed nuts, desiccated coconut

CHERRY

1 ½ cups pitted frozen cherries

1–4 tbsp milk of your choice

RASPBERRY FRO-YO

1 cup frozen raspberries

1–4 tbsp natural yogurt of
   your choice

PIÑA COLADA

1 cup frozen pineapple chunks

1–4 tbsp coconut milk

All blenders are different and some don't need much liquid at all to get the frozen fruit smooth like ice cream. Start with a small amount of liquid (1–2 tablespoons) and then add more if you find your blender isn't blending the fruit. If it ends up a little runny you can pop it back in the freezer for half an hour or so.

OTHER FRUITS THAT WORK WELL

Bananas (the classic!), blueberries, and strawberries. Experiment and mix and match! Adding half a frozen banana to any of the above recipes will make it extra creamy so try that, too!

OAT CHEWS

PREP: 5 minutes
COOK: 20 minutes
MAKES: 9 chews

Ideal first food (finger food)

These are perfect for breakfast or a snack on the go. I tend to use a mix of puffed grains for these, including whole-grain rice, buckwheat, and spelt, but feel free to mix this up depending on what is available. Buckwheat and quinoa puffs have the added benefit of providing some protein so they are worth hunting down in the store if you have the time.

For older babies and children add a couple of handfuls of dried fruit (e.g., chopped apricots, raisins, or sultanas) to the mix.

BANANA & COCONUT

2 tbsp coconut oil, plus extra for greasing
2 bananas, peeled and mashed
½ cup (15 g) puffed cereal
1 cup (80 g) oats
4 tbsp desiccated coconut

APPLE & ALMOND

2 tbsp coconut oil, plus extra for greasing
½ cup (125 g) apple sauce (see page 160)
½ cup (15 g) puffed cereal
1 cup (80 g) oats
4 tbsp ground almonds
½ tsp cinnamon

SUBSTITUTIONS

Replace the banana or apple sauce with 2 tsp pumpkin pie spice and 1 cup (200 g) butternut squash, peeled, cut into ½-inch (1 cm) squares, steamed and then mashed, for a veggie-loaded alternative.

Preheat the oven to 375°F (190°C) and grease 9 holes of a muffin pan with a little coconut oil.

Melt the coconut oil in a small saucepan. In a bowl, mix together the coconut oil with all the other ingredients. Spoon the mixture into the greased pan to about ½ inch (1 cm) thick in each hole. Press the mixture down lightly.

Bake for 20 minutes. Leave to cool completely before turning out.

The chews will keep in an airtight container for 2–3 days and they freeze well.

PEANUT BUTTER & COCONUT COOKIES

PREP: 5 minutes
COOK: 30 minutes
MAKES: 24 cookies

One 15.5-ounce (440 g) can chickpeas, drained and rinsed

1 banana, peeled and sliced

½ cup (125 g) peanut butter

¼ cup (50 g) desiccated coconut, plus more to decorate

2 tbsp coconut oil, melted

2 tbsp milk of your choice

When I was developing these cookies I tried various different things to get a texture I was happy with. In the end it was the least expected ingredient that worked the best. So I present peanut butter, coconut, and *chickpea* cookies! Yes, that's right, chickpeas are amazing in a cookie!

With chickpeas and peanut butter these cookies are packing in the protein, mono- and polyunsaturated fats, iron, and zinc. They are also great for little hands to grab so suitable for younger babies, too.

For older children (or even just for you), I'd totally recommend stirring in a handful or two of dark chocolate chunks. I tend to make half a batch without chocolate and half a batch with.

Preheat the oven to 350°F (180°C) and line a baking sheet with parchment paper.

Put all the ingredients in a blender and blend until smooth. Spoon the mixture onto the parchment paper (you need around 1½ tablespoons per cookie, to make 24). Use a fork to flatten and shape each cookie (they don't spread when cooking so try to get them to the shape you want now). Sprinkle a little more desiccated coconut on top.

Bake for about 30 minutes until the cookies are crisp and golden on top.

The cookies are best (and crunchiest) when they are first cooked. They become softer as you leave them. They'll keep for 2–3 days in an airtight container.

APRICOT & CASHEW BLISS BALLS

Apricots and tahini are both rich in calcium so this little energy ball delivers a great dairy-free dose of calcium. I haven't used much dried fruit throughout this book as it's very sweet; however, I was eager to include some apricot and these balls are too good not to include. Not an everyday recipe, but definitely a good one when you all need a little pick-me-up.

PREP: 10 minutes
(plus 1 hour to set)
MAKES: around 10 balls

12 dried apricots
½ cup (40 g) desiccated
   coconut, plus more to roll
   the balls in
½ cup (70 g) cashews
2 tbsp tahini

Put all the ingredients in a blender along with 1 tablespoon water. Blend the mix until it's fairly smooth and comes together. You might need to scrape the mix off the sides of the blender and pulse again to get everything blended well.

Put some desiccated coconut into a bowl. Roll the mixture in your hands to make about 10 balls, each about 1 inch (2.5 cm) across. Roll each ball in the coconut to coat well. Pop the balls the fridge to set for about an hour.

The balls will last around a week in the fridge, and they freeze really well, too.

TIP

Try to buy unsulfured or organic dried apricots if you can (sulfur dioxide can trigger an allergic reaction and/or digestive discomfort in some babies).

BANANA & ZUCCHINI BREAD

PREP: 10 minutes
COOK: 40 minutes
MAKES: 1 loaf or
9 muffins

Ideal first food (finger food)

1½ cups (165 g) whole wheat flour

1 tsp baking powder

1 tsp cinnamon

2 very ripe bananas

½ zucchini, grated

2 eggs (or 2 flax eggs, see page 182)

4 tbsp coconut oil, melted, plus extra for greasing, if needed

Milk of your choice, if needed

OPTIONAL EXTRAS

½ cup or 2 handfuls of any/a combination of chopped nuts, dried fruits, seeds, or fresh berries

Banana bread lasts no time at all in our house—the kids devour it. In fact, I haven't met a baby who doesn't like banana bread. This is my version, which has no added sugar (just the bananas to naturally sweeten), and the zucchini keeps it moist without being too heavy (and means it's veggie-loaded!).

As your baby gets bigger feel free to adapt this recipe and add dried fruits or fresh berries, or crushed nuts and seeds for a protein boost.

Preheat the oven to 350°F (180°C) and line an 8 × 4-inch (20 × 10 cm/450 g) loaf pan with parchment paper (or grease 9 cups of a 12-cup muffin pan if you want to make muffins).

Mix together the flour, baking powder, and cinnamon. In another bowl mash the bananas and add the grated zucchini, eggs, and coconut oil. Mix well and then add to the flour bowl and stir until incorporated. Fold in any optional extras, if using. If the mix is looking a little dry add a tablespoon or two of milk.

Pour the mixture into the pan and bake for around 40 minutes for a loaf and 20 minutes for muffins until golden on top and cooked through. If a toothpick comes out clean, then it's ready.

Remove from the oven and leave to cool for a few minutes before turning out onto a wire cooling rack.

Banana bread keeps for around 4 days in an airtight container. It also freezes well. If you want to freeze it, cut it into slices and put a little parchment paper between each slice so you can defrost a slice at a time.

VEGGIE FROM THE START

ADAPTING RECIPES

You might want to swap out various ingredients to suit your own dietary preferences, such as if you are vegan or simply if you are trying to reduce the animal products that you eat, or you may need to adapt a recipe if your baby has an allergy. This section is for parents who have had their baby's allergies confirmed. If you suspect that your baby has an allergy, see your pediatrician.

DAIRY-FREE

"Most dairy products can be swapped in recipes for dairy-free alternative products."

There are many dairy-free alternatives to milk, yogurt, cheese, sour cream, etc. Please note this section is about choosing dairy-free products for use in cooking. If your baby is over 12 months and you are looking for a dairy-free alternative to milk for them to drink please speak to your pediatrician about which milk is best.

Most dairy products can be swapped in recipes for dairy-free alternative products including soy, coconut, almond, and oat. Just be aware that this might change the flavor of a dish. I find oat-based alternatives good all around, but often use coconut products in sweet dishes.

Some products are less suitable for young children than others as they can contain ingredients that you don't necessarily want your baby to have in large quantities, like sugar and additives. Check the labels, in particular looking out for:

Sugar & salt
Try and choose products with no added salt and sugar; remember that sugar can be added in various forms. Look out for the following words:

- Words ending in "ose": e.g., glucose, sucrose, fructose, dextrose
- Dextrin and maltodextrin
- Syrups
- Honey

Ingredients on packaging are listed in order of weight, so if you see sugar and salt appear in the first few ingredients, you should avoid the product.

Emulsifiers, stabilizers & thickeners
Emulsifiers stop liquids from separating, stabilizers bind ingredients together, and thickeners do what they say! They are commonly used in dairy-free products to give a similar creamy texture and mouthfeel to dairy. Common additives are carrageenan, guar gum, and locust bean gum. These may cause digestive irritation in some cases, so you may prefer to avoid them and go for products with fewer additives.

FORTIFIED PRODUCTS

Some dairy-free products are fortified with calcium and other important nutrients found in dairy like B2, B12, vitamin D, and iodine. You can check for these added nutrients on the product's packaging.

Organic products tend not to be fortified. However, they are lower in pesticide residues and often (but not always!) contain fewer other additives. So overall it isn't always a straightforward choice between organic and nonorganic products.

CHEESE REPLACEMENTS

I've tried to list cheese as optional where it doesn't materially impact a recipe. There are lots of things you can use in the place of cheese in recipes. I have tried to list what these might be in the recipes, but here are a couple I regularly use:

Nutritional yeast
Nutritional yeast comes in flakes of deactivated yeast (they look a bit like fish food!). I really like nutritional yeast and use it a lot. It has a great "cheesy" taste and is very low in salt so it's quite good as a cheese replacement in things such as pesto to bring the salt content down. Try to buy one enriched with B12.

Toasted seeds
If you are looking for something to sprinkle over a dish as you would cheese, toasted nuts and seeds are a good option as they have lots of flavor. Blend to a powder if you have a smaller baby.

WHEAT- & GLUTEN-FREE

"Be aware that gluten-free flours may change how a recipe works."

There are now lots of different gluten- and wheat-free flours and products on the market, so if your baby has a wheat or gluten allergy you should be able to experiment and swap flours. In addition to standard gluten-free flours that you can buy, you can use buckwheat flour, oat flour, or ground almonds. Make your own oat flour by milling gluten-free oats in a blender until fine. Just be aware that gluten-free flours may change how a recipe works; baked goods like muffins are unlikely to be as fluffy, but they will still taste great.

EGG-FREE

If your baby has an egg allergy or if you are vegan then the following are good egg replacements. I've indicated on recipes which replacement works, although you can experiment, too.

BAKING/ BINDING

If you are baking, you have a couple of options to use instead of egg. I prefer to use these rather than the cartons of "egg replacement" that you can buy, which can contain lots of fillers.

"Tofu is a great direct replacement for egg."

Tofu
Tofu is a great direct replacement for egg (such as in quiche or "scrambled"). It's an excellent source of protein and calcium. I use firm tofu in the recipes (¼ cup/75 g is is about 1 egg).

Flax or chia egg
To make a flax or chia egg, mix 1 tablespoon ground flaxseeds or chia seeds with 3 tablespoons water. Stir well and leave to thicken for around 10 minutes.

Fruit
Half a banana, mashed, or ¼ cup (60 g) apple sauce (see page 160) can be used in baking in the place of 1 egg to bind a recipe. They will change the taste of the recipe and are definitely best used in sweets that are baked!

Flax or chia egg wash
An egg wash helps breadcrumbs stick if you are giving something a crunchy coating. To make an egg-free version, mix together 1 tablespoon ground flaxseeds or ground chia seeds with 2 tablespoons water. Leave the mix to thicken for 10 minutes. Then stir in 1 tablespoon plant-based milk.

NUT & SEED ALLERGIES

> "Don't feel despondent if your baby has a nut or seed allergy."

I use nuts and seeds a lot throughout this book as they are a great source of protein and fat. However, don't feel despondent if your baby has a nut or seed allergy. With a few swaps you can make most recipes nut- and/or seed-free.

There are three distinct allergies:
- Peanut
- Tree nut (e.g., walnuts, almonds, cashews, Brazil nuts, etc.)
- Seeds (e.g., sesame, pumpkin, sunflower, etc.)

If your baby is only allergic to one of the categories, or one type of nut or seed, then it's very easy to simply replace the allergenic nut in a recipe with a nut or seed that your baby is not allergic to.

There are seed spreads on the market that you can use in place of peanut or nut butter, e.g., pumpkin seed spread.

Something like hulled hemp seeds are a good replacement for cashews if your baby has a tree nut allergy but not a seed allergy.

If your baby is allergic to all nuts and seeds (or you are awaiting a detailed diagnosis so have been told to avoid all nuts and seeds in the meantime) the following are good switches to use in recipes:

FAT

Where nuts and/or seeds are adding fats to a recipe, the following are good alternatives:

- Avocado (half an avocado is equal to two handfuls of nuts/seeds)
- When the nuts/seeds are sprinkled on top to give flavor, try using cheese or nutritional yeast
- Egg (e.g., in the cashew noodles on page 132)
- Yogurt/cream cheese where they are adding creaminess such as in breakfast sushi (page 42)

PROTEIN

In baking where the nuts and/or seeds are adding protein:

- Quinoa flakes/quinoa flour
- Buckwheat flour

ALLERGY INFORMATION BY RECIPE

RECIPE	VEGAN	DAIRY FREE	EGG FREE	NUT & SEED FREE	GLUTEN FREE
Carrot cake oats (p. 39)	YES	YES	YES	OPTION	YES
Peach & almond oats (p. 39)	YES	YES	YES		YES
Carrot cake overnight oats (p. 40)	OPTION	OPTION	YES	YES	YES
Peach & almond overnight oats (p. 40)	OPTION	OPTION	YES		YES
Carrot cake oat bites (p. 41)	OPTION	OPTION	YES	YES	YES
Peach & almond oat bites (p. 41)	OPTION	OPTION	YES		YES
Breakfast sushi (p. 42)	OPTION	YES	YES	OPTION	OPTION
Buckwheat galettes (p. 43)	OPTION	YES	OPTION	YES	
Rainbow pancakes (p. 44)		YES		OPTION	OPTION
Vegan baked pancake (p. 48)	YES	YES	YES		
Coconut quinoa breakfast bowl (p. 50)	YES	YES	YES	OPTION	YES
Nut puffs (p. 51)	YES	YES	YES	OPTION	OPTION
Green smoothie (p. 53)	YES	YES	YES	YES	YES
Pink smoothie (p. 53)	YES	YES	YES		YES
Orange smoothie (p. 53)	YES	YES	YES	YES	YES
Mini egg frittata (p. 57)		OPTION		YES	YES
Mini tofu frittata (p. 57)	YES	YES	YES	YES	YES
Avocado & tahini toast (p. 58)	YES	YES	YES		OPTION
Raspberry & apple breakfast muffins (p. 60)	OPTION	YES	OPTION	OPTION	
Sweet potato rosti (p. 64)	OPTION	YES	OPTION	YES	
Green eggs (p. 65)		YES		YES	YES
Green tofu (p. 65)	YES	YES	YES	YES	YES
Beet & carrot fritters (p. 71)	OPTION	OPTION	OPTION	YES	
Sweet potato thins (p. 72)	YES	YES	YES	YES	YES
Kale, pea & buckwheat pancakes (p. 75)		OPTION		YES	YES
Protein-boosted fruit & veggies (p. 76)	OPTION	OPTION	OPTION	OPTION	YES
Cauliflower & broccoli cheese muffins (p. 80)	OPTION	OPTION	OPTION	YES	
Pumpkin, spinach & seed muffins (p. 81)	OPTION	YES	OPTION		
Savory oat bars (p. 84)		OPTION		OPTION	YES
Polenta chips (p. 88)	YES	YES	YES	YES	YES
Chickpea crackers (p. 91)	YES	OPTION	YES		YES
Pesto (p. 94)	OPTION	OPTION	YES	OPTION	YES
Basic hummus (p. 96)	YES	YES	YES	OPTION	YES
Carrot, beet, or red pepper hummus (p. 97)	YES	YES	YES		YES
Fava dip (p. 98)	YES	YES	YES	YES	YES
Tahini dip (p. 99)	OPTION	OPTION	YES		YES
Roast beet dip (p. 102)	OPTION	OPTION	YES	YES	YES
Eggplant dip (p. 103)	OPTION	OPTION	YES	YES	YES

RECIPE	VEGAN	DAIRY FREE	EGG FREE	NUT & SEED FREE	GLUTEN FREE
Cheeze sauce (p. 104)	OPTION	OPTION	YES	YES	YES
Veggie-loaded tomato sauce (p. 105)	YES	YES	YES	YES	YES
Satay bowl (p. 112)	YES	YES	YES		
Sushi bowl (p. 114)	YES	YES	YES		YES
Dukkah bowl (p. 117)		YES			
Mexican bowl (p. 118)	YES	YES	YES	YES	YES
Dal your way (p. 122)	YES	YES	YES	YES	YES
Pea orzotto (p. 124)	OPTION	OPTION	YES	OPTION	
Magic curry (p. 126)	YES	YES	YES	YES	YES
Sweet potato tostadas with black bean dip (p. 131)	YES	YES	YES	YES	YES
Cashew noodles (p. 132)	YES	YES	YES	OPTION	
Summer rolls (p. 133)	YES	YES	YES	OPTION	YES
Tarts (p. 136)	OPTION	OPTION	YES	OPTION	OPTION
Pastry parcels (p. 137)	OPTION	OPTION	YES	OPTION	OPTION
Pinwheels (p. 137)	OPTION	OPTION	YES	OPTION	OPTION
Lentil balls with tomato sauce (p. 140)	YES	YES	YES	YES	YES
Baked beans & mini potatoes (p. 142)	YES	YES	YES	YES	YES
Quinoa veggie fries & homemade ketchup (p. 145)	OPTION	YES	OPTION	YES	OPTION
One-pot veggie quinoa chili (p. 146)	YES	YES	YES	YES	YES
Vedgeree (p. 147)	OPTION	YES	OPTION	YES	YES
Quesadilla (p. 148)	OPTION	OPTION	YES	YES	OPTION
Taco bowl (p. 149)	YES	YES	YES	YES	OPTION
Pizza (p. 149)	OPTION	OPTION	YES	YES	OPTION
Mushroom (miso) broth (p. 153)	OPTION	YES	OPTION	OPTION	OPTION
Easy butternut risotto (p. 155)	OPTION	OPTION	YES	YES	YES
Sweet potato "quiche" (p. 156)	OPTION	OPTION		YES	YES
Apple sauce (p. 160)	YES	YES	YES	YES	YES
Mango & coconut ice pop (p. 161)	YES	YES	YES	YES	YES
Beet pop ice pop (p. 161)	YES	OPTION	YES	YES	YES
The hulk ice pop (p. 161)	YES	YES	YES	YES	YES
Coconut & cardamom stove-top rice pudding (p. 164)	YES	YES	YES	YES	YES
Mango chia jam (p. 166)	YES	YES	YES		YES
Quick berry compote (p. 167)	YES	YES	YES	YES	YES
Cherry nice cream (p. 169)	YES	YES	YES	YES	YES
Raspberry fro-yo nice cream (p. 169)	YES	OPTION	YES	YES	YES
Piña colada nice cream (p. 169)	YES	YES	YES	YES	YES
Banana & coconut oat chews (p. 171)	YES	YES	YES	YES	YES
Apple & almond oat chews (p. 171)	YES	YES	YES		YES
Peanut butter & coconut cookies (p. 172)	YES	YES	YES		YES
Apricot & coconut bliss ball (p. 174)	YES	YES	YES		YES
Banana & zucchini bread (p. 176)	OPTION	YES	OPTION	YES	

RESOURCES

CLIMATE CHANGE

The EAT-Lancet Commission on Food, Planet, Health

eatforum.org/eat-lancet-commission/ (Full report: Food in the Anthropocene: the EAT–Lancet Commission on healthy diets from sustainable food systems, vol. 393, issue 10170, 447–92, 2019)

WEANING & NUTRITION

Healthychildren.org, from the American Academy of Pediatrics: Guidance on starting solid foods

healthychildren.org/English/ages-stages/baby/feeding-nutrition/Pages/Starting-Solid-Foods.aspx

The American Academy of Pediatrics

aap.org/en-us/advocacy-and-policy/aap-health-initiatives/HALF-Implementation-Guide/Age-Specific-Content/Pages/Infant-Food-and-Feeding.aspx

Centers for Disease Control and Prevention (CDC)

cdc.gov/nutrition/InfantandToddlerNutrition/foods-and-drinks/index.html

FOOD LABELS

FDA guidance on reading nutrition labels

fda.gov/food/new-nutrition-facts-label/how-understand-and-use-nutrition-facts-label

VEGETARIAN & VEGAN DIETS

The Vegetarian Resource Group

vrg.org

The Academy of Nutrition and Dietetics guidance on vegetarian and vegan diets

eatright.org/food/nutrition/vegetarian-and-special-diets/feeding-vegetarian-and-vegan-infants-and-toddlers

BUYING IN SEASON

Seasonal food guide by state

seasonalfoodguide.org

Center for Urban Education about Sustainable Agriculture: seasonality chart

cuesa.org/eat-seasonally/charts/vegetables

INDEX

Page references in *italics* indicate images.

ACKNOWLEDGMENTS

This book was commissioned when my third child was two weeks old. Writing a cookbook has been the fulfillment of a dream for me, but it's fair to say that writing a book with a newborn wasn't always plain sailing. It involved a lot of support (emotional and practical!) from a lot of people—I am grateful to you all.

Thank you so much to Sam and Emma at Vermilion for making this happen. And to the rest of the team behind the design, editing, and proofreading—thank you for making the book what it is.

To the amazing photography team who brought the food to life: my good friend Tania for taking the photos—and for believing in the project (and me!) right from the start. To Kitty and Bobbi for directing the props, cooking, styling, and making the food look so delicious! And of course the fantastic models: my own children, Tom and Jon, and the amazing babies Chloe, Hattie, Jesse, and Roman (and their parents!).

Thank you to consultant nutritionist and friend Jodie Abrahams for answering hundreds of my questions, for all your support and enthusiasm throughout.

This book would never have happened without my community on Instagram—to everyone who has cooked my recipes, supported me, asked me questions and liked my posts. To the "Instagram friends": the ones I've never met, and the ones I have.

Thank you to the wonderful group of recipe testers who took the time to cook the recipes and give me detailed feedback—it was all invaluable. Especially baby Mini for being my chief recipe tester and giving true, age-appropriate feedback during the test phase.

I am so grateful to my family for instilling in me a love of food—in particular my sister Becky, my aunt Liz and my late grandmother Rossi. My dad Michael for his excitement throughout and for reading his first ever cookbook (and for giving me all the lessons in grammar—turns out it's never too late to learn new things!). And my mum Sheila, for always insisting we sit at the dinner table and showing me the importance of every family meal.

This book would not have been possible without the support of my husband Rob. Thanks for putting up with me!

And last but most definitely not least, my three children. Felix for giving me the idea to set up Little Veggie Eats in the first place. Juno for inheriting my unquestioning love of food. And finally Coco for being the type of baby you can write (and shoot!) a book around.

ABOUT THE AUTHOR
AND CONTRIBUTOR

Rachel Boyett posts her family veggie and vegan recipes on her popular Instagram @littleveggieeats and blog littleveggieeats.com. She is a mother of three and a lifetime vegetarian.

When she started weaning she quickly realized that rather than being an extra level of work, weaning was actually really fun and a great opportunity to get creative. Her own style of cooking and recipes has evolved as her family has grown and now she's a firm believer in one meal for all the family.

Jodie Abrahams (MBANT, CNHC) is a registered nutritionist. Jodie speaks, writes, and consults on nutrition and also works one-to-one with clients as a nutritional therapist. She is based in East London and has two children.

Jodie is passionate about making good nutrition accessible, achievable, and enjoyable for all.

jodieabrahams.com